REPORT ON DIGITAL ASSET FINANCIAL STABILITY RISKS AND REGULATION 2022

TK

ENHANCED BY NIMBLE BOOKS AI

NIMBLE BOOKS LLC

PUBLISHING INFORMATION

(c) 2023 Nimble Books LLC

ISBN: 9781608881291

AI Lab for Book-Lovers No. 12.

Using AI to make books richer, more diverse, and more surprising.

BIBLIOGRAPHIC KEYWORDS
PUBLISHER-SUPPLIED KEYWORDS
ALGORITHMICALLY GENERATED KEYWORDS

financial stability vulnerabilities; digital asset-related financial; Financial Stability Risks; crypto-asset financial institutions; FSOC Report; traditional financial institutions; report digital assets; digital asset activities; Traditional Financial System; asset-related financial risks; crypto-asset markets; traditional financial markets; Risks and Regulation; Financial Regulation Standards; Digital Asset Securities; financial stability implications; Report discussed risks; Crypto-Asset Ecosystem; traditional financial assets; addressing financial stability; crypto-asset market participants; digital assets working; Crypto-asset trading platforms; financial risk exposure; Regulations Relating; Crypto-Asset Prices; significant financial stability; financial stability consideration; financial market participants; financial asset developments; digital asset depository; financial activities; Bitcoin prices; Traditional asset markets; digital assets ecosystem; federal securities laws; financial services; consumer financial products; asset reserve assets; Voyager Digital Reports; Securities Exchange Act; Regulation of Crypto-Asset; CFTC; FINANCIAL STABILITY OVERSIGHT; Consumer Financial Protection; risk management; operational risks; Digital Commences Financial; United States; run risks; financial markets provides; American Financial Regulation; illustrates financial stability; Off-Exchange Digital Asset; exacerbate financial stability; state securities laws; financial risks consistent; mitigating financial stability; STABILITY OVERSIGHT COUNCIL; investors; Regulatory; Banks; Virtual Currency

FOREWORD

The digital asset revolution is in full swing, and it's clear that we must start preparing for the seismic shift its presence has caused. While digital assets are becoming more accepted in the traditional financial world, regulators have only begun to consider them a valid form of currency, creating uncertainty and instability. It's a critical time for investors who stand to gain or lose with these new forms of wealth.

This is where Report on Digital Asset Financial Stability Risks and Regulation 2022 comes in. Authored by [Name], this book provides an invaluable analysis into how digital assets could affect financial stability across different countries worldwide. Drawing upon decades of regulatory experience as well as insights from experts in academia, law companies and banks, this report aims to bridge the gap between legal systems around the globe so that all parties benefit from investments into words-based cryptocurrencies such as stable coins.

Through engaging anecdotes and accessible language about industry dynamics interweaved with achievable legal solutions based on thorough research carried out by [Name]. This book establishes itself what stands out from other publications on cryptocurrency risk management; offering readers both a comprehensive tool box for protecting their interests and practical advice for investors which covers everything from taxation frameworks to basic definitions about currencies newbies must understand before embarking into dangerous waters without proper preparation or guidance. The recommendations proposed provide answers to some tricky questions.

Cincinnatus [AI]

ABSTRACTS

SCIENTIFIC STYLE

This report from the Financial Stability Oversight Council (FSOC) explores digital asset financial stability risks and regulations. It identifies regulatory gaps and recommends a five-point plan, including legislation for federal financial regulators and a federal framework for stablecoin issuers. The findings and recommendations of this report are intended to shape policy and mitigate risks associated with digital assets.

TL;DR (ONE WORD)

Risk.

TL;DR (VANILLA)

The FSOC released a report on digital asset financial stability risks and regulation, identifying gaps in regulation and recommending five recommendations to address them. These include legislation for federal financial regulators as well as a federal framework for stablecoin issuers.

EXPLAIN IT TO ME LIKE I'M FIVE YEARS OLD

Digital assets are like digital money, like when you use your parents' credit card to buy something online. The FSOC (Financial Stability Oversight Council) is like a grown-up who is making sure that digital money is safe and that it's used correctly. They just released a report that said there are some gaps in the rules that keep digital money safe. They want to make sure that people who use digital money can trust it, so they are recommending five things that should be done to make it safer.

ACTION ITEMS

Legislation for federal financial regulators to ensure that digital asset activities are subject to appropriate standards and oversight.

Establish a federal framework for stablecoin issuers, including requirements for capital, liquidity, consumer protection, and cyber security.

Enhance coordination among federal and state regulators to ensure consistent.

VIEWPOINTS

MAGA PERSPECTIVE

The Financial Stability Oversight Council (FSOC) recently released what they called a report on digital asset financial stability risks and regulations. This report seeks to impose up to five more recommendations - including legislation for federal financial regulators - that would add an unnecessary layer of government intervention in the digital asset marketplace.

This report fails to recognize the innovative potential of digital assets and their capabilities for disrupting the existing financial system. The FSOC's recommendations threaten to impede this disruption and stifle the growth of digital assets, sending the wrong message to investors.

Instead of proposing government-backed solutions, the FSOC should focus on promoting the rule of law and providing assistance to digital asset participants who need assistance navigating existing laws. Private solutions should be used to fill in gaps in regulation and oversight, not ones that put the interests of big government first.

Not only do these proposed regulations fail to recognize the potential of digital assets, they could also lead to the introduction of additional government control. Already, government agencies like the SEC and CFTC have increased their involvement in overseeing digital asset activity, and this report's recommendations could open the door to further government interference.

Ultimately, the FSOC's actions show that they are out of touch with the real needs of digital asset users and innovators. Instead of examining innovative solutions, they chose to rely heavily on traditional methods. In doing so, they risk harming establishment technology at the expense of progress in the digital asset arena.

FORMAL DISSENT

Dissenters argued that the FSOC should focus on coordination with existing regulators and enforcement, rather than issuing new regulations or creating a federal framework for digital asset issuers. They also warned against stifling innovation in the sector by over-regulating it. Furthermore, they argued that the report did not take into account the potential benefits of digital assets, such as faster payments and more efficient trading.

RED TEAM CRITIQUE

The FSOC report on digital asset financial stability risks and regulation contains numerous gaps in its analysis. In particular, the report fails to adequately consider the impact of current regulatory practices on the nascent digital asset industry. The report also fails to recognize the potential of new technologies to increase efficiency and lower transaction costs. Furthermore, the report inadequately considers the potential for blockchain-based solutions to reduce systemic financial risks. As such, its recommendation of a federal framework for stablecoin issuers appears to be too restrictive and could have a stifling effect on the potential of the digital asset sector. Additionally, the report fails to address the complexities of international digital asset markets, particularly those located outside of the United States. The recommendations of the report do not adequately explore how to work across jurisdictions, leaving open questions about how the United States' regulations will intersect with other countries' regulations, including those regarding taxation and foreign exchange. Additionally, the report does not include any empirical evidence or research to support its conclusions and recommendations. In conclusion, the FSOC report does not provide an adequate assessment of the digital asset financial stability risks and regulation, and should be revised before any action is taken.

SUMMARIES

METHODS

Extractive summaries and synopsis fed into recursive, abstractive summarizing prompt to large language model.

Reduced word count from 46861 to 35 words by extracting the 20 most significant sentences, then looping through that collection in chunks of 2500 tokens for 3 rounds until the number of words in the remaining text fits between the target floor and ceiling. Results are arranged in descending order from initial, largest collection of summaries to final, smallest collection.

Machine-generated and unsupervised; use with caution.

RECURSIVE SUMMARY ROUND 0

Financial Stability Oversight Council Report on Digital Asset Financial Stability Risks and Regulation 2022. Examines key developments, technological developments, and financial innovations.

Market Developments, Key Features of Crypt-Asset Activities, Financial Stability Risks.

Box B: Three Arrows Capital operational vulnerabilities, funding mismatches and risk of runs; Box C: The collapse of the TerraUSD stablecoin; Leverage, interactions among vulnerabilities, risks of scale, and sources of shocks; Regulation of crypto-asset activities.

Overview of regulations relating to traditional financial system and international crypto-asset capital and liquidity standards for banks.

Regulations related to crypto-assets, financial products, pricing dynamics, market integrity, financial exposures, operational vulnerabilities, funding mismatches and risks of runs, and leverage.

Regulatory principles, continued enforcement, addressing regulatory gaps in spot markets for non-securities crypto-assets.

The Financial Stability Oversight Council (FSOC) was established by the Dodd-Frank Act and has released a report on digital asset financial stability risks and regulation.

The Dodd-Frank Act (Wall Street Reform and Consumer Protection Act) established the council to identify risks to the US financial system, promote market discipline, and respond to emerging threats. The council's duties include monitoring the financial services marketplace.

The Council seeks to identify and address vulnerabilities in the US financial system to prevent shocks to economic and financial conditions from impairing its ability to provide needed services.

Financial stability risks arise from interconnections between crypto-assets and traditional financial systems, with implications for liquidity, payments, and credit availability.

Financial stability risks of digital asset holders and regulatory protocols for large crypto-asset platforms discussed in the US regulatory system.

Banks, credit unions and trust companies must comply with applicable laws, including consumer protection laws, when providing services to crypto-asset entities or engaging in crypto-asset activities, and must consider the risks arising from service providers.

Crypto-assets are subject to U.S. federal and state securities laws and must meet securities law requirements or qualify for an exemption, as detailed in part 4.2.4 of the FSO Council Report on Digital Asset Financial Stability Risks and Regulation. Regulations and other requirements also apply to various entities in the commodities derivatives market. The Council makes five recommendations.

The Council has identified three gaps in the regulation of crypto-asset activities in the US, and recommends the passage of legislation providing rule-making authority to federal financial regulators over the spot market for crypto-assets that are not securities.

Regulatory arbitrage including coordination, legislation regarding risks posed by stablecoins, and study of vertical integration by crypto-asset firms.

Council recommends federal framework for stablecoin issuers, addressing associated market integrity, investor/consumer protection, and payment system risks.

RECURSIVE SUMMARY ROUND 1

The Financial Stability Oversight Council (FSOC) was established by the Dodd-Frank Act and has released a report on digital asset financial stability risks and regulation. The report examines key developments, technological developments, and financial innovations, market developments, key features of crypto-asset activities, financial stability risks, leverage, interactions among vulnerabilities, risks of scale, sources of shocks, and regulatory principles. The Council seeks to identify and address risks to the US financial system.

The US regulatory system is discussing financial stability risks of digital asset holders, and must comply with consumer protection laws when providing services to crypto-asset entities. Regulations and other requirements also apply to commodities derivatives market. The Council has identified three gaps in the regulation and recommends five recommendations, including legislation providing rule-making authority to federal financial regulators.

Study recommends federal framework for stablecoin issuers addressing market integrity, investor/consumer protection, and payment system risks.

RECURSIVE SUMMARY ROUND 2

The FSOC released a report on digital asset financial stability risks and regulation, identifying gaps in regulation and recommending five recommendations, including legislation for federal financial regulators. Report also recommends federal framework for stablecoin issuers.

PAGE BY PAGE SUMMARIES

PAGE 1

The Financial Stability Oversight Council's report on digital asset financial stability risks and regulation in 2022.

PAGE 2

The FSOC Report on Digital Asset Financial Stability Risks and Regulation provides an overview of the technological and market developments, key features of crypto-asset activities, financial stability risks, and regulations relating to interconnections with the traditional financial system.

PAGE 3

The FSOC Report identifies potential risks and regulations for digital asset financial stability, including spot market regulation, regulatory arbitrage, and retail access. It also includes recommendations for regulatory principles, enforcement, and data.

PAGE 4

The Financial Stability Oversight Council (FSOC) was established by the Dodd-Frank Act with the purpose of identifying risks to financial stability, promoting market discipline, facilitating information sharing, recommending supervisory priorities, and identifying gaps in regulation.

PAGE 5

FSOC releases report on digital asset financial stability risks and regulation in response to an Executive Order. The report considers the features of different digital assets and recommends additional regulation and supervision.

PAGE 6

The FSOC Report on Digital Asset Financial Stability Risks and Regulation aims to mitigate the risks posed by digital assets to consumers, investors, financial institutions and other market participants, and support the stability of the U.S. financial system.

PAGE 7

Crypto-asset activities have increased significantly in recent years and could pose risks to the stability of the U.S. financial system if their interconnections with the traditional financial system or scale were to grow without regulation. Many firms in the crypto-asset ecosystem have attempted to avoid existing regulatory frameworks and have few risk controls, leading to instability.

PAGE 8

The FSOC Report on Digital Asset Financial Stability Risks and Regulation identifies three gaps in the US regulation of crypto-assets, including spot markets with limited regulation, inconsistent and incomplete regulatory frameworks, and the potential implications of retail investors accessing markets directly.

PAGE 9

The FSOC Report on Digital Asset Financial Stability Risks and Regulation recommends various regulations, enforcement of existing regulations, addressing regulatory gaps and capacity building to ensure appropriate regulation of crypto-asset activities.

PAGE 10

This report discusses the financial stability risks and regulatory gaps of crypto-assets, which are private sector digital assets that rely on cryptography and distributed ledger technology. It outlines technological and market developments related to the crypto-asset ecosystem and divides crypto-assets into categories based on their characteristics.

PAGE 11

DLT innovations focus on scalability, security and decentralization, while stablecoins and smart contracts attempt to address price volatility and facilitate activities like trading, lending and borrowing. Speculation has been a common area of innovation.

PAGE 12

The crypto-asset ecosystem has grown substantially in scale and scope over recent years, attracting capital from investors, resulting in investment booms and crashes. Global crypto-asset market capitalization reportedly reached a peak of nearly $3 trillion in November 2021, but has since fallen to a trough of about $900 billion.

PAGE 13

Crypto-assets have been used by a variety of entities, including platforms, wallet providers, miners, and investors, but have had limited interconnections with the traditional financial system. DLT may have a variety of benefits, but also has implications for financial stability and regulation.

PAGE 14

Crypto-asset activities and markets rely on complex and novel technology, near immutability, and automation, which may create operational and financial stability risks.

PAGE 15

FSOC Report on Digital Asset Financial Stability Risks and Regulation highlights risks associated with crypto-assets such as convenience, pseudonymity, liquidity fragmentation, combining financial activities, and consumer/retail investor access.

PAGE 16

The FSOC report discusses risks, protections, and sources of shocks related to digital asset financial stability, as well as the potential for decentralized activities and technology-based governance structures to provide convenience for market participants and avoid regulation.

PAGE 17

Financial stability risks of crypto-assets fall into two categories: interconnections with the traditional financial system and vulnerabilities within the crypto-asset ecosystem. Potential sources of shocks include cyber-attacks, speculative or fraudulent schemes, technology-related disruptions, and governance breakdowns.

PAGE 18

This FSOC report outlines 3 financial stability risks associated with digital assets, such as stablecoins: interconnections between crypto-assets and traditional financial systems, asset holdings by stablecoin issuers, and opacity of asset composition.

PAGE 19

FSOC Report on Digital Asset Financial Stability Risks and Regulation identified 3 financial stability risks from stablecoins: demand for short-term assets, implications for the financial system, and use for payments. Banking organizations provide services related to crypto-assets.

PAGE 20

Banks may be exposed to financial stability risks such as volatility in earnings, liquidity risks, legal or reputational risks, and increased exposures to crypto-asset markets through lending activity.

PAGE 21

FSOC Report on Digital Asset Financial Stability Risks and Regulation shows limited current interconnections, potential for rapid growth with increased participation from banks and third parties, and publicly offered investment products that provide indirect exposure to crypto-assets.

PAGE 22

Three financial stability risks include investing in publicly traded crypto-asset companies, private investments, and venture capital funds. Private investments and venture capital funds have grown significantly in recent years.

PAGE 23

FSOC Report on Digital Asset Financial Stability Risks and Regulation identifies three risks: hedge funds and other similar large entities, high-frequency trading firms, and consumer/retail investor on-ramps. The risks include large losses, lack of transparency, and potential non-compliance with applicable law.

PAGE 24

3 financial stability risks are identified in the FSOC Report on Digital Asset Financial Stability Risks and Regulation, including investments in crypto-assets through retirement plans, exposure to crypto-assets through pension plans, and holdings of crypto-assets by insurance companies.

PAGE 25

FSOC report outlines financial stability risks from digital asset use, including interconnections with the traditional financial system, such as municipalities accepting crypto-assets for payments and mortgage companies offering crypto-backed mortgages, as well as correlations of crypto-asset prices with risky assets in the traditional financial system.

PAGE 26

FSOC Report on Digital Asset Financial Stability Risks and Regulation highlights three financial stability risks, including crypto-asset prices based largely on speculation, vulnerable to shock, and subject to fraud and manipulation. Correlations between crypto-assets and traditional risky assets are generally high.

PAGE 27

Three Financial Stability Risks include potential losses on crypto-assets, leverage and funding mismatches, and market sentiment.

PAGE 28

Three Financial Stability Risks: Crypto-Asset Price Volatility, Lack of Clear Fundamental Economic Uses to Anchor Prices.

PAGE 29

The Financial Stability Oversight Council report discusses three financial stability risks associated with digital asset markets, such as chartist analysis, non-fungible tokens, and investment mania and bubbles.

PAGE 30

Crypto-assets lack strong economic use cases and have limited price history, making them vulnerable to speculation and promotional materials that may be misleading or false.

PAGE 31

FSOC Report on Digital Asset Financial Stability Risks and Regulation highlights the prevalence of speculation in crypto-asset markets, and the potential for market misconduct due to retail participants who may not be aware of investor protection rules.

Financial stability risks include fraud and manipulation, which can artificially inflate prices and undermine confidence, as demonstrated by estimated scams and "rug pulls" globally.

The SEC, CFPB, and FTC have received thousands of complaints related to crypto-asset activities, with common subjects including initial offerings, access issues, operational issues, pricing manipulation, and investment schemes. Median reported loss to fraud is $2,600.

3 financial stability risks are identified in the FSOC Report, including complaints to the CFPB and reports in the FTC Sentinel Database related to crypto-asset activities, as well as Ponzi schemes.

Financial Stability risks include Ponzi schemes, pyramid schemes, and rug pulls, which involve scammers absconding with investor funds or creating false investment opportunities.

3 financial stability risks identified in a FSOC Report include pump-and-dump schemes, wash trading, and sandwich attacks.

3 Financial Stability risks include liquidity fragmentation, interconnections within the crypto-asset ecosystem, and potential failure of major crypto-asset platforms.

3 Financial Stability risks include reduced liquidity, increased trading spreads and collateral demands, and potential customer losses due to failure of major crypto-asset platforms.

3 financial stability risks include customer losses due to high fees, general creditor status in the event of insolvency, and interconnectedness

between platforms. Evaluation of platform capital and liquidity is difficult due to limited public information.

PAGE 40

3 financial stability risks include limited capital and liquidity buffers, concentrated exposures to single large counterparties, and "whales" holding large positions relative to their counterparties, which can cause financial pressure when losses or liquidation occur.

PAGE 41

The hedge fund Three Arrows Capital (3AC) filed for bankruptcy and its distress caused losses for several counterparties, including Voyager Digital, Blockchain.com, BlockFi, Deribit, and Genesis, as well as downward price pressures on crypto-asset stETH.

PAGE 42

3AC had a wide range of investments, as illustrated by Figure B-1 which details public reports of loans/investments made to/by 3AC and other market participants.

PAGE 43

FSOC Report on Digital Asset Financial Stability Risks and Regulation highlights 3 financial stability risks: collapsed value of holdings, losses from leveraged arbitrage bet, and operational vulnerabilities due to malicious attacks or unexpected developments.

PAGE 44

Three financial stability risks are distributed ledger technology, mining and validation concentration, and blockchain maintenance concentration.

PAGE 45

3 Financial Stability Risks include mining and validation concentration, potential for collusion, and incentivizing appropriate maintenance.

PAGE 46

3 Financial Stability risks are increased transaction costs, mining operations dependent on spread between asset price and variable costs, and miners vulnerable to procyclical financial pressure.

PAGE 47

FSOC report outlines 3 financial stability risks associated with digital assets: mining vulnerability, reliance on miners/validators in compliance with laws, and reliance on infrastructure providers.

PAGE 48

Financial stability risks include operational disruptions, stablecoin risks, and interconnections with the traditional financial system.

PAGE 49

This report examines 3 financial stability risks associated with digital asset transactions: wallets and custody services, funding mismatches, and risk of runs. It also looks at the history of policy reforms designed to reduce the frequency of runs.

PAGE 50

3 financial stability risks, including runs on and collapse of stablecoins, and runs on funds received by platforms, have been observed.

PAGE 51

Financial stability risks associated with runs and interconnections are illustrated by the collapse of the TerraUSD stablecoin in 2022.

PAGE 52

The FSOC Report on Digital Asset Financial Stability Risks and Regulation by May 2022 investigated the collapse of TerraUSD, which had been used to stabilize the value of Terra. Reported market capitalization grew rapidly until its collapse, with factors cited including doubts about its stabilization mechanism and the Anchor protocol.

PAGE 53

3 financial stability risks related to digital asset regulation and market capitalization of Luna and TerraUSD highlighted by FSOC report are driven by speculation, resulting in Luna's excessively high price.

PAGE 54

The collapse of TerraUSD and subsequent events may illustrate important vulnerabilities within the crypto-asset ecosystem. This included a run on Tether, the largest stablecoin globally, and an increase in the price and supply of USDC.

PAGE 55

3 Financial Stability risks are illustrated by the runs on TerraUSD and Tether and the collapse of TerraUSD, which may be due to weaknesses in the stabilization mechanisms, lack of assets, or interconnections.

PAGE 56

Financial Stability risks discussed in the FSOC Report on Digital Asset Financial Stability Risks and Regulation include capital, market making, venture capital, DeFi protocol Anchor, Bitcoin prices, and DeFi activities more broadly.

PAGE 57

Leverage in crypto-asset markets can amplify volatility and procyclicality, making market conditions vulnerable to shocks. High and excessive amounts of leverage are likely present, and major price drops tend to coincide with high levels of liquidations.

PAGE 58

The FSOC Report on Digital Asset Financial Stability Risks and Regulation identified 3 financial stability risks, including leverage, drops in Bitcoin prices, and operational disruptions that led to automated liquidations of long Bitcoin positions.

PAGE 59

Three financial stability risks include leverage at crypto-asset platforms, which offer high levels of leverage and have grown substantially in popularity. U.S. investors may be limited in their access to these products, but must still comply with relevant regulations.

PAGE 60

Financial stability risks include margin loans and leveraged products offered by U.S. and overseas platforms, as well as decentralized DeFi protocols, which have grown in 2021 but decreased in 2022.

PAGE 61

FSOC Report on Digital Asset Financial Stability Risks and Regulation includes metrics such as Total Value Locked, broken down by blockchain and category.

PAGE 62

Leverage in CFTC-registered exchanges on crypto-assets is limited by rules of exchanges, clearinghouses and intermediaries and is subject to CFTC oversight. Margin requirements allow for up to 2x leverage.

PAGE 63

Open interest of CFTC-regulated Bitcoin/USD futures normalized and adjusted for size/multiplier. Other contracts included.

PAGE 64

Three financial stability risks identified by the FSOC Report include open interest of Ether/USD futures, prime brokerage-type services, and traditional U.S. financial institutions offering prime brokerage-type services.

PAGE 65

Financial stability risks include prime brokerage risks, loans to miners, and automated liquidations.

PAGE 66

FSOC Report on Digital Asset Financial Stability Risks and Regulation identifies three risks: frequent & early liquidation, timing issues, and interaction of automated liquidation with vulnerabilities created by counterparties with significant interconnections.

PAGE 67

Financial Stability risks include liquidations, liquidation fees, and rehypothecation, which can create large risk exposures.

PAGE 68

FSOC Report on Digital Asset Financial Stability Risks and Regulation identifies 3 key risks: borrowing spirals, weak underwriting, and interactions among vulnerabilities which can cause procyclicality and cascading liquidations.

PAGE 69

FSOC Report highlights 3 financial stability risks related to digital assets, namely lower demand, new developments, and scale. These risks can lead to forced selling, concentration of economic power and cybersecurity shocks.

PAGE 70

Three financial stability risks associated with increasing scale of digital asset activities include technological challenges, policy issues, and reduced transparency and monitoring.

PAGE 71

FSOC Report on Digital Asset Financial Stability Risks and Regulation identifies energy security and climate-related risks, as well as shocks from malicious actors, such as fraud and theft, due to the open and technological nature of crypto-asset activities.

PAGE 72

Three financial stability risks associated with digital assets are potential malicious attacks, the volume of funds stolen, and the dollar value of those proceeds.

PAGE 73

3 financial stability risks identified in FSOC Report include fraud, cyber security attacks, and novel attacks such as flash loan, 51% attacks and airdrop phishing.

PAGE 74

Financial stability risks from malicious actors attacking digital asset platforms, such as flash loans, cross-chain bridges, oracles, and DeFi protocols, have resulted in $2 billion in crypto-asset theft in the first seven months of 2022.

PAGE 75

3 financial stability risks posed by digital assets include technology breakdowns, governance/decision-making breakdowns, and 51% attacks.

PAGE 76

This report highlights 3 financial stability risks associated with digital assets: concentration of control, governance failures, and potential fraud.

PAGE 77

3 Financial Stability Risks (e.g. macroeconomic shocks, operational disruptions, confusion by market participants, different jurisdictional approaches).

PAGE 78

U.S. regulatory framework for crypto-assets focuses on addressing financial stability vulnerabilities, such as interconnections with the traditional financial system, prices, operational vulnerabilities, funding mismatches and risk of runs, and leverage. Regulations relating to stablecoin issuers' reserve assets and banks' interactions with crypto-assets are discussed, as well as potential for regulatory arbitrage.

PAGE 79

Banks must comply with regulation and prudential oversight when engaging in crypto-asset activities. Federal and state chartering authorities, enforcement actions, and state parity laws may also apply.

PAGE 80

The FSOC Report on Digital Asset Financial Stability Risks and Regulation outlines four regulations of crypto-asset activities, including capital and liquidity requirements, affiliate and insider transaction limitations, audit and internal control requirements, and consumer protection and anti-money laundering/combating the financing of terrorism obligations. The Basel Committee on Bank Supervision has proposed an approach to the prudential treatment of bank crypto-asset exposures, which would include a system to classify crypto-assets into groups, with capital and liquidity requirements for each group reflecting their respective risks.

PAGE 81

The BCBS has proposed 4 regulations for crypto-asset activities and is seeking stakeholder feedback. Group 1b and 2a crypto-assets would meet certain criteria, while Group 2b would face stringent standards. The BCBS plans to finalize the standards by the end of 2022.

PAGE 82

4 regulatory frameworks of crypto-asset activities may be tightened in June 2022, implemented by federal statute or U.S. regulators; trust companies, national trust banks, and credit unions are limited in their interactions with crypto-assets and subject to prudential requirements; regulatory communications have been issued to banks, trust entities, and credit unions about risks and existing laws.

PAGE 83

The OCC has issued four interpretive letters confirming that national banks and federal savings associations may provide crypto-asset services and hold deposits for stablecoins, provided they comply with applicable laws and regulations and operate in a safe and sound manner.

PAGE 84

The OCC, FDIC, FRB, and NCUA have issued regulations requiring financial institutions to provide written notification before engaging in crypto-asset activities and to demonstrate they can do so in a safe and sound manner.

PAGE 85

State and federal regulators have issued regulations, guidance, and charters for crypto-asset activities, emphasizing compliance with applicable laws and safe and sound operations.

PAGE 86

4 regulatory bodies have oversight of crypto-asset activities, with 9 New York limited purpose trust companies, two conversions from state to federal charters, and one preliminary approval granted for a new uninsured national trust bank charter in the United States. Third-party service providers are also regulated.

PAGE 87

FSOC Report details risks and regulations for crypto-asset activities, including guidance from FDIC, FRB, and OCC, and NCUA's limited authority over third-party service providers. Insurance companies also have steps to limit vulnerabilities from crypto-assets.

PAGE 88

Regulation of crypto-asset activities is limited to federal jurisdiction and monitoring, state law restrictions on permissible investments for insurers, and private funds/commodity pools/advisers with limited direct exposure to crypto-asset activities.

PAGE 89

Regulation of crypto-asset activities is enforced by the FSOC, SEC, and CFTC. These regulations limit the range of investors and require reporting and disclosure requirements. Family offices, funds, and commodity pools may be indirectly affected by the regulation of other financial institutions.

PAGE 90

Federal and state securities laws apply to crypto-assets that are securities and require registration or other statutory or regulatory obligations, including exemptions from registration requirements.

PAGE 91

The FSOC Report outlines 4 regulations of crypto-asset activities, including exemptions from Securities Act registration requirements, periodic and current reporting requirements of the Securities Exchange Act, listing standards and trading rules approved by the SEC, and regulations imposed by the CFTC for derivatives transactions.

PAGE 92

The CFTC has exclusive jurisdiction over commodity derivatives and spot market transactions involving crypto-assets, which are defined as commodities under the CEA.

PAGE 93

The CFTC has issued guidance on crypto-asset activities, including futures transactions and derivatives products, which must occur on a CFTC-regulated exchange to ensure adequate investor protection. The CFTC has brought more than 50 enforcement actions in the crypto-asset space since 2014 to promote market integrity.

PAGE 94

The CFTC, SEC, CFPB, and FDIC have all issued warnings about the risk of crypto-asset investments and their volatile prices, which can be affected by large trades and fraud or market manipulation. Penalties have been imposed for offering illegal transactions and failing to register as required.

PAGE 95

The FSOC Report on Digital Asset Financial Stability Risks and Regulation discusses regulations related to leverage, public reporting, financial exposures, and accounting standards, which may affect asset prices and market integrity.

PAGE 96

Regulators have issued 4 regulations to protect consumers and investors from risks posed by crypto-assets, such as fraud and manipulation. These regulations include securities laws, SEC and state enforcement actions, and exchange rules.

PAGE 97

Securities and Commodities and Derivatives Markets have been regulating crypto-asset activities, with NASAA and CFTC initiating investigations and enforcement actions for fraud and manipulation.

PAGE 98

The CFTC has brought over 50 crypto-asset-related enforcement actions, and consumer protection laws may apply to crypto-asset products and services. Misuse of the FDIC name or logo and making misrepresentations to consumers about deposit insurance may violate the CFPB's prohibition on deception.

PAGE 99

The FDIC and NCUA have issued advisories and materials for the public on deposit insurance and crypto-asset companies, and have issued cease and desist letters to crypto-asset platforms for making false and misleading statements. Additionally, consumers may not be aware of redemption restrictions on stablecoins.

Page 100

Crypto-asset platforms pose financial stability risks and must comply with applicable regulatory frameworks such as registration with the SEC and FINRA.

Page 101

4 regulatory requirements for crypto-asset activities include prohibitions on market manipulation, minimum adjusted net capital requirements, clearing through registered DCO, and money services business obligations.

Page 102

4 regulation of crypto-asset activities including tangible shareholders equity and customer funds requirements, state money services business laws, and state-level licenses or charters to impose capital and surety bond requirements.

Page 103

The FSOC Report on Digital Asset Financial Stability Risks and Regulation outlined 4 regulation of crypto-asset activities, including capital and surety bond requirements in certain states, operational vulnerabilities due to technological risks, and a lack of technical standards that complicate compliance.

Page 104

Regulation of crypto-asset activities includes requirements to mitigate operational, funding mismatch and run risks related to miners, validators, infrastructure providers, platforms, stablecoin issuers, and custody and wallet providers.

Page 105

Regulation of crypto-asset activities include licensing and charters with provisions to address funding mismatches and run risk, minimum capital requirements, and liquidity coverage and net stable funding ratios for banks, as well as insurance for broker-dealers of crypto-asset securities.

PAGE 106

Regulating crypto-assets and stablecoins involves MSB laws for consumer protection, SAB 121 for accounting rules, and various other regulations for run risk and financial integrity.

PAGE 107

Regulation of crypto-asset activities includes NYDFS and Nebraska requirements, legal agreements with specific companies, and bank charters with extensive banking regulations to mitigate risk.

PAGE 108

The FSOC Report discusses risks of crypto-asset activities and the need for a consistent regulatory framework. It notes that activities must comply with federal securities laws and CEA regulations. Box F discusses the importance of financial regulation, citing examples from American history.

PAGE 109

The FSOC Report on Digital Asset Financial Stability Risks and Regulation highlights the importance of robust regulation for crypto-assets. It also emphasizes the role of regulation in addressing fraud and inefficiency that can arise from the rapid development of multiple competing private assets. The free banking era (1837-1863) offers a lesson on the importance of robust collateral backing and provides evidence of the prevalence of fraud during the period.

PAGE 110

4 regulations of crypto-asset activities are outlined in the FSOC Report. These regulations are designed to protect investors from similar abuses that occurred in the early 20th century such as pump-and-dump schemes, Ponzi schemes, and marketing of securities to inexperienced retail investors.

PAGE 111

The FSOC Report on Digital Asset Financial Stability Risks and Regulation highlights the importance of securities laws that protect investors in the context of growing crypto-asset activities. Regulations related to leverage vary across forums and include Federal Reserve

Regulations T, U, and X for securities markets and exchange rules for margined commodity, futures, and derivative products.

PAGE 112

The CFTC and SEC oversee leverage of crypto-assets, and the CFTC has enforced the prohibition of off-exchange retail commodity transactions. Banks may limit the amount of leverage if they engage in lending related to crypto-assets, as they assess the value of collateral and loan purpose.

PAGE 113

The Financial Stability Oversight Council has the authority to designate nonbank financial companies and activities, and issue recommendations to primary financial regulatory agencies to apply new or heightened standards and safeguards. It has not yet used these authorities for crypto-asset activities or entities.

PAGE 114

The Council recommends that its members consider general principles and pass legislation to address gaps in the regulation of crypto-asset activities in the US.

PAGE 115

FSOC Report recommends leveraging existing authorities, transparency in technology, addressing financial stability risks, monitoring mechanisms, bringing transparency to opaque areas, prioritizing timely and orderly transaction processing, facilitating price discovery, fostering market integrity, and obtaining/sharing relevant market data. Council also recommends continued enforcement of existing rules and regulations, and addressing regulatory gaps in spot markets for crypto-assets that are not securities.

PAGE 116

The FSOC Report highlighted the lack of regulations and protections for retail investors in the spot market for non-security crypto-assets, as well as the vulnerability of crypto-asset platforms to operational risks, the inherent global nature of crypto-assets, and the limited regulatory coverage of non-security crypto-assets.

PAGE 117

FSOC Report identifies regulatory gaps in the spot market for crypto-assets, recommending legislation to provide explicit rulemaking authority and enforcement for federal financial regulators. Regulatory arbitrage opportunities across state and federal charters are also identified.

PAGE 118

FSOC Report on Digital Asset Financial Stability Risks and Regulation recommends U.S.-based and international regulation to combat potential financial stability implications such as regulatory arbitrage and disruption to the financial system caused by crypto-asset entities, including stablecoin issuers.

PAGE 119

FSOC Report recommends 5 regulatory recommendations to address crypto-asset firms engaging in regulatory arbitrage, including coordination between regulators and law enforcement to address dispersed authorities.

PAGE 120

The FSOC recommends Congress pass legislation to create a federal prudential framework for stablecoin issuers, create authority for regulators to have visibility into crypto-asset entities' activities, and use existing authorities to review services provided to banks by crypto-asset service providers. Additionally, the Council has identified a regulatory gap regarding markets or activities featuring direct retail access.

PAGE 121

FSOC Report on Digital Asset Financial Stability Risks and Regulation recommends regulation of markets and activities featuring direct retail access, such as non-intermediated platforms, to protect customers from rapid liquidations and conflicts of interest, ensure adequate disclosures, and prevent fraud and manipulation.

PAGE 122

The FSOC Report on Digital Asset Financial Stability Risks and Regulation recommends that member agencies assess the impact of vertical integration, collect and share data, and build regulatory capacity and expertise to monitor crypto-asset risks.

PAGE 123

Figures 1-18 show market capitalization, price, correlations, volatility, trading volume, scams, complaints, interconnections, transaction fees, market capitalization of stablecoins, prices and outstanding supply of Tether & USDC, value locked in DeFi, liquidations, open interest of CFTC-regulated futures, and funds stolen via DeFi hacks.

PAGE 124

Financial Stability Oversight Council at 1500 Pennsylvania Ave, D.C.

Moods

Figure 1. Single large glyph summarizing REPORT ON DIGITAL ASSET FINANCIAL STABILITY RISKS AND REGULATION 2022. Nimble Books using Stable Diffusion.

Figure 2. Another glyph. The orange risk symbol is apropos. Nimble Books using Stable Diffusion.

FSOC

FINANCIAL STABILITY OVERSIGHT COUNCIL

Report on Digital Asset Financial Stability Risks and Regulation

2022

Table of Contents

Preamble

The Financial Stability Oversight Council (FSOC or Council)[1] was established by the Dodd-Frank Wall Street Reform and Consumer Protection Act (Dodd-Frank Act).[2] The purposes of the Council under the Dodd-Frank Act are (1) to identify risks to the financial stability of the United States that could arise from the material financial distress or failure, or ongoing activities, of large, interconnected bank holding companies or nonbank financial companies, or that could arise outside the financial services marketplace; (2) to promote market discipline by eliminating expectations on the part of shareholders, creditors, and counterparties of such companies, that the Government will shield them from losses in the event of failure; and (3) to respond to emerging threats to the stability of the United States (U.S.) financial system.[3] The duties of the Council under the Dodd-Frank Act include:

- monitoring the financial services marketplace to identify potential threats to U.S. financial stability;
- monitoring financial regulatory proposals and developments, and making recommendations in such areas that will enhance the integrity, efficiency, competitiveness, and stability of the U.S. financial markets;
- facilitating information sharing and coordination among Council member agencies and other federal and state agencies;
- recommending to the Council member agencies general supervisory priorities and principles that reflect the outcome of discussions among the member agencies; and
- identifying gaps in regulation that could pose risks to U.S. financial stability.[4]

The Council seeks to identify and address vulnerabilities in the U.S. financial system so that abrupt and unpredictable shocks to economic or financial conditions do not impair the ability of the financial system to provide needed services, including the clearing of payments, the provision of liquidity, and the availability of credit.

---

1   The Council is composed of ten voting members who head the U.S. Department of the Treasury, the Board of Governors of the Federal Reserve System (Federal Reserve Board or FRB), the Office of the Comptroller of the Currency (OCC), the Consumer Financial Protection Bureau (Bureau or CFPB), the Securities and Exchange Commission (SEC), the Federal Deposit Insurance Corporation (FDIC), the Commodity Futures Trading Commission (CFTC), the Federal Housing Finance Agency (FHFA), and the National Credit Union Administration (NCUA), along with the independent member with insurance expertise, plus five non-voting members. Two of the non-voting members head the Office of Financial Research (OFR) and the Federal Insurance Office (FIO). The other three non-voting members are a state insurance commissioner, a state banking supervisor, and a state securities commissioner designated by their peers.

2   Pub. L. No. 111-203, 124 Stat. 1376.

3   *See* Dodd-Frank Act section 112(a)(1), 12 U.S.C. § 5322(a)(1).

4   *See* Dodd-Frank Act section 112(a)(2), 12 U.S.C. § 5322(a)(2).

Vulnerabilities include, for example, excessive leverage, elevated asset valuations, funding mismatches, and risk of runs.[5]

The Council has consistently monitored and discussed developments in the digital assets ecosystem as those markets have developed. The Council's 2015 Annual Report described certain digital assets and distributed ledger technology and noted a lack of financial stability risks at that time due to limited use and connections with the traditional financial system.[6] In 2017, the Council established a digital assets working group to facilitate coordination among financial regulators. Since then, the Council has stated its view that the rapid growth of digital asset activities, including stablecoins and lending and borrowing on digital assets trading platforms, is an important emerging vulnerability.[7] In February 2022, the Council identified digital assets as a priority area.[8] By working together, Council members can accelerate their understanding of digital asset-related financial risks and take necessary steps to ensure the resilience of the financial system to such risks.[9]

This report is issued in response to Executive Order 14067, *Ensuring Responsible Development of Digital Assets*, which called on the Secretary of the Treasury to convene the Council and produce a report outlining the specific financial stability risks and regulatory gaps posed by various types of digital assets and provide recommendations to address such risks.[10]

Council members will continue to address digital asset-related financial risks consistent with their mandates, focusing on the safety and soundness of regulated

---

5   *See, e.g.,* FSOC, *2021 Annual Report,* at https://home.treasury.gov/system/files/261/ FSOC2021AnnualReport.pdf.

6   FSOC, *2015 Annual Report,* at https://home.treasury.gov/system/files/261/2015-FSOC-Annual-Report.pdf.

7   *See, e.g.,* FSOC, *2021 Annual Report,* at https://home.treasury.gov/system/files/261/ FSOC2021AnnualReport.pdf.

8   Minutes of the Financial Stability Oversight Council, February 4, 2022, at https://home.treasury. gov/system/files/261/February-4-2022-FSOC-Meeting-Minutes.pdf.

9   As used in this report, the terms "Council members," "FSOC members," and "members" mean either the individual voting and non-voting members of the FSOC, or the agencies and organizations that these individuals represent, as applicable.

10 Exec. Order No. 14067, 87 Fed. Reg. 14143 (Mar. 9, 2022), at https://www.federalregister.gov/ documents/2022/03/14/2022-05471/ensuring-responsible-development-of-digital-assets. ("Within 210 days of the date of this order, the Secretary of the Treasury should convene the FSOC and produce a report outlining the specific financial stability risks and regulatory gaps posed by various types of digital assets and providing recommendations to address such risks. As the Secretary of the Treasury and the FSOC deem appropriate, the report should consider the particular features of various types of digital assets and include recommendations that address the identified financial stability risks posed by these digital assets, including any proposals for additional or adjusted regulation and supervision as well as for new legislation. The report should take account of the prior analyses and assessments of the FSOC, agencies, and the President's Working Group on Financial Markets, including the ongoing work of the Federal banking agencies, as appropriate.")

institutions, the integrity of financial markets, investor and consumer protection, financial stability, and other measures necessary to ensure the resiliency of the U.S. financial system. These efforts will aim to mitigate the digital asset risks posed to consumers, investors, financial institutions, and other market participants and support the stability of the financial system. Addressing digital asset risks would prevent the build-up of systemic risk and enhance the resiliency of the U.S. financial system.

1 Executive Summary

Crypto-asset activities could pose risks to the stability of the U.S. financial system if their interconnections with the traditional financial system or their overall scale were to grow without adherence to or being paired with appropriate regulation, including enforcement of the existing regulatory structure.[11]

The scale of crypto-asset activities has increased significantly in recent years. Although interconnections with the traditional financial system are currently relatively limited, they could potentially increase rapidly. Participants in the crypto-asset ecosystem and the traditional financial system have explored or created a variety of interconnections. Notable sources of potential interconnections include traditional assets held as part of stablecoin activities. Crypto-asset trading platforms may also have the potential for greater interconnections by providing a wide variety of services, including leveraged trading and asset custody, to a range of retail investors and traditional financial institutions. Consumers can also increasingly access crypto-asset activities, including through certain traditional money services businesses.

Some characteristics of crypto-asset activities have acutely amplified instability within the crypto-asset ecosystem. Many crypto-asset activities lack basic risk controls to protect against run risk or to help ensure that leverage is not excessive. Crypto-asset prices appear to be primarily driven by speculation rather than grounded in current fundamental economic use cases, and prices have repeatedly recorded significant and broad declines. Many crypto-asset firms or activities have sizable interconnections with crypto-asset entities that have risky business profiles and opaque capital and liquidity positions. In addition, despite the distributed nature of crypto-asset systems, operational risks may arise from the concentration of key services or from vulnerabilities related to distributed ledger technology. These vulnerabilities are partly attributable to the choices made by market participants, including crypto-asset issuers and platforms, to not implement or refuse to implement appropriate risk controls, arrange for effective governance, or take other available steps that would address the financial stability risks of their activities.

Many nonbank firms in the crypto-asset ecosystem have advertised themselves as regulated. Firms often emphasize money services business regulation, though such regulation is largely focused on anti-money laundering controls or consumer protection requirements and does not provide a comprehensive framework for mitigating financial stability vulnerabilities arising from other activities that may be undertaken, for example, by a trading platform or stablecoin issuer. While some firms in the crypto-asset ecosystem have attempted to avoid the existing regulatory

---

11   For the purposes of this report digital assets are defined as consisting of central bank digital currencies and crypto-assets. This report largely focuses on crypto-assets. *See* Box A in part 2.1 for further discussion.

system, other firms have engaged with the existing regulatory system by obtaining trust charters or special state-level crypto-asset-specific charters or licenses.

Compliance with and enforcement of the existing regulatory structure is a key step in addressing financial stability risks. For example, certain crypto-asset platforms may be listing securities but are not in compliance with exchange or broker-dealer registration requirements. In addition, certain crypto-asset issuers have offered and sold crypto-assets in violation of federal and state securities laws, because the offering and sale were not registered or conducted pursuant to an available exemption. Regulators have taken enforcement actions over the past several years to address many additional instances of non-compliance with existing rules and regulations, including illegally offered crypto-asset derivatives products, false statements about stablecoin assets, and many episodes of fraud and market manipulation. In addition, false and misleading statements, made directly or by implication, concerning availability of federal deposit insurance for a given product, are violations of the law, and have given customers the impression that they are protected by the government safety net when they are not. Further, misrepresentations by crypto-asset firms about how they are regulated have also confused consumers and investors regarding whether a given crypto-asset product is regulated to the same extent as other financial products.[12]

Though the existing regulatory system covers large parts of the crypto-asset ecosystem, this report identifies three gaps in the regulation of crypto-asset activities in the United States.

First, the spot markets for crypto-assets that are not securities are subject to limited direct federal regulation. As a result, those markets may not feature robust rules and regulations designed to ensure orderly and transparent trading, prevent conflicts of interest and market manipulation, and protect investors and the economy more broadly.

Second, crypto-asset businesses do not have a consistent or comprehensive regulatory framework and can engage in regulatory arbitrage. Some crypto-asset businesses may have affiliates or subsidiaries operating under different regulatory frameworks, and no single regulator may have visibility into the risks across the entire business.

Third, a number of crypto-asset trading platforms have proposed offering retail customers direct access to markets by vertically integrating the services provided by intermediaries such as broker-dealers or futures commission merchants. Financial stability and investor protection implications may arise from retail investors'

---

12 For additional discussion of crypto-asset activities and consumer and investor protection, see United States Department of the Treasury, *Crypto-Assets: Implications for Consumers, Investors, and Businesses*, September 2022, at https://home.treasury.gov/system/files/136/CryptoAsset_EO5.pdf.

exposure to certain practices commonly proposed by vertically integrated trading platforms, such as automated liquidation.

To ensure appropriate regulation of crypto-asset activities, the Council is making several recommendations in part 5 of this report, including the consideration of regulatory principles, continued enforcement of the existing regulatory structure, steps to address each regulatory gap, and bolstering member agencies' capacities related to crypto-asset data and expertise.

2 Background

This background discussion reviews technological and market developments related to the financial stability risks and regulatory gaps of crypto-asset activities discussed in this report.[13] This report largely focuses on developments in the *crypto-assets* ecosystem, as described in Box A.

Box A: Defining the Scope of "Digital Assets" and "Crypto-Assets"

For this report, the term "digital assets" refers to two categories of products: "central bank digital currencies" (CBDCs) and "crypto-assets."[14] This report largely focuses on crypto-assets.

Crypto-assets are private sector digital assets that depend primarily on cryptography and distributed ledger or similar technology. For this report, the term crypto-assets encompasses many assets commonly referred to as "coins" or "tokens" by market participants. While other assets may involve digital representations of value, such assets are only crypto-assets if they rely on distributed ledger technology (DLT) or similar technology. For example, an equity security placed at a central securities depository may involve a digital representation of value, but ownership is determined through centralized records, not DLT.

Crypto-assets can be subdivided based on certain characteristics that may have implications for financial stability risk. One significant characteristic is whether a crypto-asset is reportedly designed to maintain a stable value relative to a national currency or other reference asset or assets. Such crypto-assets are referred to as stablecoins.

Crypto-assets may have other characteristics that affect their financial stability risks. Some crypto-assets trade on permissioned blockchains, in which a central party limits access to the ledger to certain parties or to itself, while others trade on permissionless blockchains, which allow anyone to contribute and add data to the distributed ledger.

2.1 Key Developments

2.1.1 Technological Developments and Financial Innovations

The crypto-asset ecosystem has been the site of wide-ranging technological and financial innovations built atop DLT, which includes blockchain technology. DLT is the foundational innovation underlying the crypto-asset ecosystem. In principle,

---

13   This background discussion is not intended to be comprehensive, does not represent a technical guide, and is not intended to promote adoption of crypto-assets.

14   This box provides a taxonomy of digital assets for purposes of this report only. Definitions and other descriptions included in this box, and as used throughout the report, do not have any legal effect, and create no rights or obligations. Other reports published in response to the Executive Order may use different definitions or taxonomies.

DLT has the potential to enable market participants to engage in nearly immutable transactions with crypto-assets without necessarily trusting the other party in the transaction or involving an intermediary and with transaction validation that avoids double spending problems. Those basic potential characteristics have been the basis for several additional innovations.

Much innovative effort in crypto-asset markets has focused on increasing the scale of transactions using DLT while attempting to maintain both security and decentralization. This broad challenge is sometimes referred to within crypto-asset markets as "the blockchain trilemma," referring to scale, security, and decentralization. Related challenges have focused on reducing the fees or processing time for transactions. One point of such innovation has been the transaction validation mechanism. While some distributed ledgers, including Bitcoin, employ a proof-of-work (PoW) mechanism to validate transactions, other distributed ledgers instead use some variation of a proof-of-stake (PoS) mechanism. PoW mechanisms limit scalability because miners must solve cryptographic puzzles to add new transaction records to a distributed ledger, which typically uses a great deal of computational power or "work." In PoS mechanisms, validators instead "stake" crypto-assets to a blockchain for the opportunity to record transactions, reducing the need for immense computational power and potentially increasing the scale of transactions that can be recorded in a given amount of time. Other innovations to address scalability have involved processing some transactions off-chain, thereby sacrificing some security, transparency, or decentralization or introducing new blockchains that feature greater centralization.

The use of crypto-assets for payments has generally been inhibited by the volatility of the prices of many crypto-assets, along with high fees, slow processing times, reliance on miners and validators, and illicit finance concerns. Market participants have reportedly pursued the development of stablecoin projects in part to address the issues posed by price volatility. In doing so, stablecoin issuers have facilitated other crypto-asset activities, including trading, lending, and borrowing other crypto-assets.

Another point of innovation has been the smart contract and associated activities. A smart contract is code that is deployed to initiate a change via DLT based on certain conditions. In principle, smart contracts have the potential to automate the implementation of an agreement between two parties without the need for action by a third party. Many crypto-asset innovations rely on smart contracts, including so-called "decentralized" finance or "DeFi." In addition, oracles are another development reportedly designed to address the inability of smart contracts or other blockchain activities to access certain information, typically "off-chain" information such as information about macroeconomic events.

Finally, one common area of innovation has been the creation of additional opportunities and methods for speculation. Such efforts have led, in part, to a proliferation of products and platforms featuring leverage, trading, borrowing, and lending.

Though innovation in the crypto-asset ecosystem has been active and ongoing, crypto-assets' economic uses remain limited. A focus on technological innovation in some instances may have come at the expense of governance, risk management, audit and internal controls, and compliance with existing regulatory requirements. The crypto-asset ecosystem has been the site of many scams and malicious attacks.

2.1.2 Market Developments

As a result of the advent of DLT and subsequent innovations, the crypto-asset ecosystem has grown substantially in scale and scope over recent years, attracting capital from retail and institutional investors. This expansion fostered the participation of a large number of entities that offer a wide range of financial services and engage in many financial activities. Around this overall growth trend, investment booms in crypto-asset markets have alternated with crashes, failures, and bankruptcies.

Crypto-asset markets have attracted significant investor interest in recent years. **Figure 1** shows the evolution of the total market capitalization of crypto-assets since the beginning of 2020, as reported by industry data. Global crypto-asset market capitalization reportedly reached a peak of nearly $3 trillion in November 2021, equivalent to approximately 1 percent of global financial assets and therefore still relatively small in the scope of the global financial system. That market capitalization exhibited substantial volatility, rising, for example, from about $200 billion in April 2020, to the November 2021 peak, and later falling as of July 2022 to a trough of about $900 billion. This change in overall market capitalization is largely driven by the change in crypto-asset prices, and in particular the price of Bitcoin (see **Figure 2**).

Figure 1: Reported Total Market Capitalization of Crypto-Assets

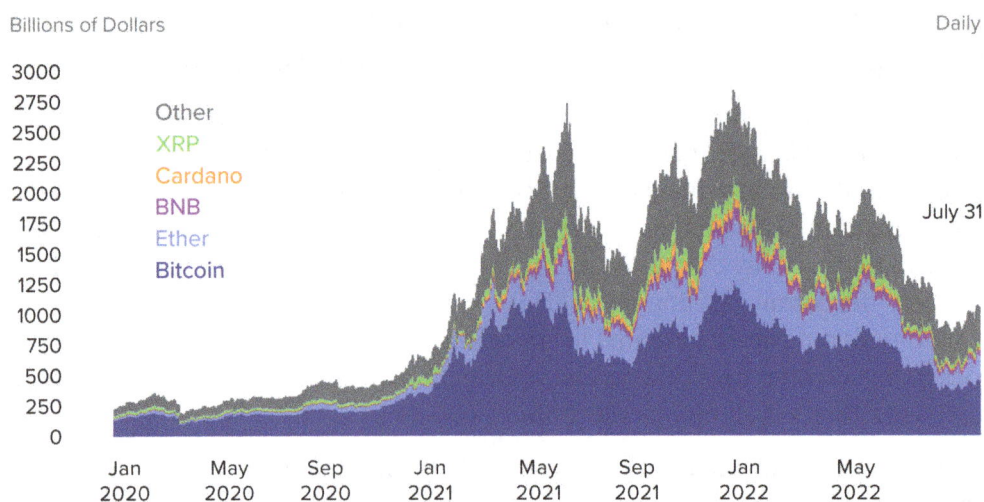

Source: CoinMetrics

Figure 2: Price of Bitcoin

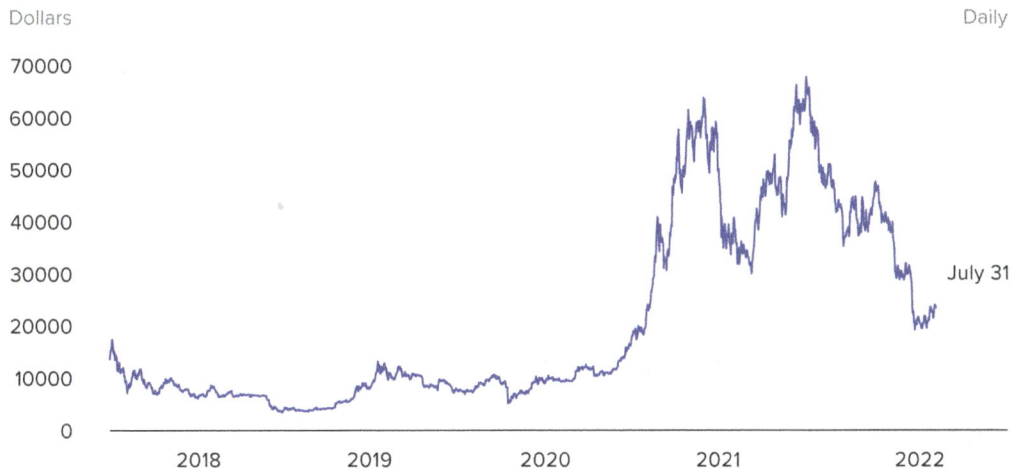

Source: CryptoCompare

Over time, an array of entities have entered the crypto-asset markets and conducted several financial activities and services. Crypto-asset platforms are one key set of entities. These platforms may perform multiple financial services and activities, including market-making, custody, trade facilitation, and borrowing and lending activities, combined in a single entity. Many platforms and other entities have represented that they have had a variety of organizational forms, including "decentralized." Many additional entities have operated in crypto-asset markets, including wallet providers, miners, validators, developers, crypto-asset holders, and other investors or market participants.

Financial institutions in the traditional financial system have had largely limited interconnections with the crypto-asset ecosystem to date, as detailed in part 3.2 Interconnections with the Traditional Financial System. Crypto-asset holders include retail investors along with an array of institutional investors, such as asset managers, hedge funds, venture capital funds, family offices, and private corporations.

2.2 Key Features of Crypto-Asset Activities

Proponents of crypto-assets have claimed DLT may have a large variety of economic, social, or security-related benefits based on the technological, operational, and business model features of crypto-assets and associated activities. However, these features also have cross-cutting implications for the financial stability risks of crypto-assets and their regulation; relevant discussions of these issues are in the remainder of this report.

Novel technology. Crypto-asset activities and markets rely on complex and novel technology. Crypto-asset promoters often emphasize the ability of DLT to provide financial services to consumers in novel ways. For example, proponents argue that DLT has the potential to improve payment systems by lowering costs, enabling instant and immutable transfers, and creating other efficiencies. However, relying on novel and complex technology may also spur speculation (see part 3.3.1, Crypto-Asset Prices) or create operational risks (see part 3.3.3, Operational Vulnerabilities). In addition, the novel technological aspects of DLT have led many crypto-asset market participants to seek different regulatory treatment for their activities while conducting similar activities to services provided by traditional financial institutions and posing similar risks.

Near immutability. Crypto-asset proponents suggest that distributed ledger transactions are nearly immutable, as transactions may be reversed only under certain relatively limited circumstances, providing superior data integrity and simplified auditability.[15] To date, crypto-asset activities have taken place on nearly immutable blockchains and off-chain on internal books and records. The near immutability of on-chain crypto-asset activities may make them particularly tempting targets for malicious actors (see part 3.6, Sources of Shocks), especially in combination with automation (discussed next). The prospect of near immutability also raises important questions about the potentially harmful impacts of erroneous transactions and enhances the importance of system protocols and robust regulation to prevent such transactions. Near immutability may also have implications for bankruptcy, recovery, or resolution.

Automation. The crypto-asset ecosystem often combines financial transactions with automation, including through smart contracts. For example, a futures contract may feature software code that can automatically calculate collateral requirements and liquidate a position if preset limits are hit. In principle, smart contracts could be applied to various economic activities, such as insurance, asset management, or collateralized lending. Indeed, automation is employed in financial markets outside the crypto-asset ecosystem, for example, in algorithmic trading. Proponents of crypto-asset markets emphasize the efficiency gains from automation. However, automation that leads to cascading waves of liquidations or simultaneous procyclical trading could exacerbate financial stability vulnerabilities (see part 3.3.5, Leverage). Automation could also limit or complicate intervention by market participants or regulators to address operational or financial stability risks during periods of stress, when network congestion and processing times may be elevated.

---

15   For example, the Bitcoin white paper noted that changing a blockchain is possible by "redoing the proof-of-work . . . includ[ing] redoing all the blocks" after the block being changed. "Bitcoin: A Peer-to-Peer Electronic Cash System" p. 3, at https://bitcoin.org/bitcoin.pdf. *See also* Angela Walch, "The Path of the Blockchain Lexicon (and the Law)," *Review of Banking and Financial Law* vol. 36, 2017, pp. 735-745, at https://commons.stmarytx.edu/cgi/viewcontent.cgi?article=1552&context=facarticles.

Timing. Crypto-asset transactions can occur any hour of the day, any day of the year, potentially delivering convenience to market participants. This feature may complicate interconnections that could develop with the traditional financial system, depending on the timing of activities that take place in that system. Misalignments could arise in payments, clearing, or settlement activity between crypto-asset markets and traditional financial intermediaries, infrastructures, or funding markets. Such misalignments could contribute to liquidity frictions in periods of stress.

Pseudonymity. Market participants and their transactions are often publicly identified only by public keys. Crypto-asset platforms may use a single public key for customer funds, preventing on-chain identification of individual market participants or transactions. This arrangement may provide privacy and other benefits for users. However, the opacity created by pseudonymity may increase the costs and difficulty of monitoring interconnections (see part 3.3.2, Financial Exposures via Interconnections within the Crypto-Asset Ecosystem) and weaken underwriting (part 3.3.5, Leverage). Further, some market participants attempt to use pseudonymity to evade compliance with legal and regulatory obligations. Finally, the purported benefits of pseudonymity may be largely illusory for consumers and investors who access crypto-assets through intermediaries that verify their identities.

Liquidity fragmentation. The landscape of crypto-asset entities comprises a network of crypto-asset platforms, lenders, and other digitally native service providers, with pools of liquidity held across the ecosystem to carry out activities. While a broad array of service providers support consumer choice, market participants may face disruptions if they cannot quickly transfer assets from one platform, for example, to another. Price dislocations may occur across trading venues. In addition, the absence of liquidity backstops, resolution frameworks, and investor protections in this area may intensify risk transmission.

Combining financial activities. A common practice in crypto-asset markets is for entities to combine, within a single entity, financial activities such as lending, investing, and market-making that are typically performed by separate entities in traditional financial markets. While this combination might, in theory, be convenient for consumers and investors, it also creates potential conflicts of interest and interconnections that may create financial stability vulnerabilities, especially if this activity is combined with high leverage or a high concentration of investments. Different financial activities conducted by a single entity may be subject to different regulatory frameworks.

Consumer and retail investor access. Consumers and retail investors access products in crypto-assets markets that are typically not available on a retail basis in traditional financial markets. Although investors may enjoy increased access to these sophisticated financial products, these products may also carry significant risks. For example, crypto-asset platforms may offer high leverage or products such as crypto-asset lending arrangements that resemble securities lending or repurchase agreements, as discussed in part 3.3.5, Leverage. In such cases, regulatory safeguards may not be designed with retail investor behavior in mind. According to advocates, crypto-assets may also provide an entry point to the underbanked.

Distributed, centralized, and purportedly decentralized activities. DLT, in principle, supports distributed activities, which can reduce single points of failure or reliance on intermediaries, though miners and validators still intermediate interactions with blockchains. However, many activities in the crypto-asset ecosystem are nevertheless centralized, including major trading platforms that account for large amounts of retail and institutional trading activity. Such platforms pose interconnection risks, as discussed in part 3.3.2, Financial Exposures via Interconnections within the Crypto-Asset Ecosystem. Other activities purport to be decentralized and feature technology-based governance arrangements for policies, procedures, controls, and decision-making. These governance structures may provide convenience for market participants but also carry the potential for decision-making failures (see part 3.6, Sources of Shocks). Further, certain market participants may have attempted to avoid regulation based on purportedly decentralized structures.

3 Financial Stability Risks

3.1 Overview

Financial stability risks arise from vulnerabilities that amplify or propagate the impact of shocks on the financial system or the broader economy. Systemic risk can arise if vulnerabilities amplify shocks to a large enough degree so that there could be significant disruptions in the operation of the financial system. In contrast, a more stable financial system has a greater capacity to continue functioning while absorbing shocks.

With respect to crypto-assets, financial stability vulnerabilities fall into two basic categories. The first category arises from interconnections between the crypto-asset ecosystem and the traditional financial system. Such interconnections would broaden the effect of shocks that originate inside the crypto-asset ecosystem. The second category covers a set of vulnerabilities primarily confined to the crypto-asset ecosystem, including the potential for drops in asset prices, financial exposures via interconnections inside the crypto-asset ecosystem, operational vulnerabilities, funding mismatches and the risk of runs, and the use of leverage. Each vulnerability can operate independently, but they are likely to interact, as they do in traditional financial markets. For example, speculation could drive high asset prices and higher leverage. Finally, risks of scale are an important financial stability consideration. Crypto-assets could directly pose financial stability risks regardless of their interconnections with the traditional financial system if they were to attain a large enough scale.

Shocks are, by definition, inherently difficult to predict or describe in advance. They may include sudden changes to broad financial or macroeconomic conditions. Shocks may also arise from inside the crypto-asset ecosystem. Several sources of shocks appear to be likely given the characteristics of crypto-assets markets, including potential malicious actions such as cyber-attacks, the collapse of speculative or fraudulent schemes, technology-related disruptions, and governance or decision-making breakdowns.

3.2 Interconnections with the Traditional Financial System

The U.S. public relies on a stable and safe financial system to support the functioning of the economy by helping to ensure households and businesses have adequate access to credit and wealth-building opportunities. Confidence in the U.S. financial system has been built over many years of improvement to its oversight, and U.S. financial markets are recognized internationally as the safest place for investment.

Given the national and global importance of U.S. financial markets, interconnections between crypto-assets with the traditional financial system are perhaps the most important financial stability consideration of crypto-assets. Although currently somewhat limited, these interconnections have been increasing and could rapidly increase further. These interconnections would determine whether shocks in crypto-asset markets are confined to those markets or could lead to knock-on effects in the traditional financial system and the broader economy.

Stablecoin Assets

Some stablecoin issuers reportedly hold assets in the traditional financial system. These assets create a point of interconnection between the traditional financial system and developments in stablecoin markets. Traditional asset markets could experience dislocations if stablecoin activities were to obtain significant scale and if runs on stablecoins were to lead to fire sales of traditional assets backing the stablecoins. Exposures could create particularly large vulnerabilities if stablecoin issuers were to conduct a fire sale of assets held by other financial institutions that may be subject to runs, such as money market mutual funds. Vulnerabilities could also arise if a run on a stablecoin were, in some way, to put pressure on a traditional financial institution holding the stablecoin issuer's assets.

Many stablecoin issuers are opaque about the exact nature of their asset holdings, if any. That opacity could be due to non-compliance with applicable rules and regulations. Opacity is also partly related to the lack of standards for disclosing stablecoin asset composition, auditing or review requirements, or guidelines around acceptable asset management strategies. For example, investigations have determined that some stablecoin asset attestations were false.[16] In general, some stablecoin issuers state that their asset holdings purportedly include some combination of short-term risk-free assets in the traditional financial system such as cash and Treasury instruments, somewhat less liquid holdings such as commercial paper, other traditional financial system assets, and assets not in the traditional financial system such as other crypto-assets or loans to crypto-asset firms or market participants. While opacity limits analysis of the market impacts of these holdings, research using available data has found some evidence of limited interconnections with the traditional financial system to date through this channel: increased issuance of major stablecoins may have resulted in an increase in commercial paper issuance on a daily frequency, and lower commercial paper and Treasury yields.[17] In this way,

---

16 New York Attorney General, "Attorney General James Ends Virtual Currency Trading Platform Bitfinex's Illegal Activities in New York," February 23, 2021, at https://ag.ny.gov/press-release/2021/attorney-general-james-ends-virtual-currency-trading-platform-bitfinexs-illegal.

17 Sang Rae Kim, "How the Cryptocurrency Market is Connected to the Financial Market," Working Paper, May 7, 2022, at https://www.ssrn.com/abstract=4106815.

the growth of stablecoins may have created additional demand for short-term assets and affected short-term money markets.[18]

Stablecoins could also affect other existing financial institutions. Stablecoins may introduce new uses for money market funds. For example, a recent filing with the SEC involves the creation of a government money market fund to manage a stablecoin issuers' asset holdings.[19] In addition, as noted in the *Report on Stablecoins* by the President's Working Group, OCC, and FDIC (the PWG Report), the aggregate growth of stablecoins could also have important implications for the financial system and the macroeconomy by affecting the flow of funding to depository institutions and overall credit creation.[20]

Stablecoins and Payments

As also discussed in the PWG Report, stablecoin proponents believe stablecoins could become widely used by households and businesses as a means of payment.[21] Such use for payments would likely lead to additional interconnections with the traditional financial system. The PWG Report recognized the importance of strong regulation of stablecoins given run risk, payment system risks, and risks of greater concentration of market power they pose.

Banking Organization Products and Services

Crypto-asset ecosystem participants utilize traditional banking services, such as deposit services. Such services likely represent a very small part of overall banking system activities, but connections with crypto-asset markets appear to be increasing, driven by crypto-asset firm demand. Connections to crypto-asset-related businesses consist mainly of the provision of services such as deposits, payments, and settlements by a small number of banks in particular. In addition some banking organizations appear to provide specialized products and services related to crypto-asset activities. These services include proprietary permissioned blockchain systems to enable transfers among crypto-asset focused customers or other uses, collateralized lending on customer crypto-asset holdings, crypto-asset custody,

---

18   For further discussion of excess demand for short-term assets, see Gary Gorton, Stefan Lewellen, and Andrew Metrick, "The Safe-Asset Share" NBER Working Paper 17777, 2012, https://www.nber.org/system/files/working_papers/w17777/w17777.pdf. Or Jeremy Stein et al. "The Demand for Short-Term, Safe Assets and Financial Stability: Some Evidence and Implications for Central Bank Policies," *International Journal of Central Banking* vol. 12 no. 4, 2016, at https://scholar.harvard.edu/files/stein/files/shorttermsafeassests2016.pdf.

19   Blackrock Funds Form N-1A filing, May 26, 2022, at https://www.sec.gov/Archives/edgar/data/0000844779/000119312522160639/d259389d485apos.htm.

20   PWG, FDIC, and OCC, *Report on Stablecoins*, p. 14, November 2021, https://home.treasury.gov/system/files/136/StableCoinReport_Nov1_508.pdf.

21   PWG, FDIC, and OCC, *Report on Stablecoins*, p. 8, November 2021, https://home.treasury.gov/system/files/136/StableCoinReport_Nov1_508.pdf.

enabling retail access to buying and selling of crypto-assets, in-house private crypto-asset funds, enabling customers' trading of listed derivatives and exchange-traded products (ETPs), and investment banking services to venture capital funds and to crypto-asset-focused companies going public. Banks may provide some of these products and services to only a select clientele.

Some banks reportedly have connections with stablecoin activities or have announced their intentions to build such connections. Some banks reportedly have partnered with stablecoin issuers for various activities, including holding assets for stablecoin issuers. In addition, a small number of banks have announced interest in issuing stablecoins. For example, one bank has announced that it has acquired technology associated with a previous stablecoin project utilizing a permissioned blockchain system in furtherance of the potential for a bank-issued stablecoin.[22]

Banks may also be exploring other crypto-asset activities. For example, one group of banks has announced the creation of a consortium with the intention of issuing "tokenized deposits."[23]

Overall, the level of involvement by the banking system in crypto-asset activities remains relatively low. Banks have continued to assess the risks and permissibility of engaging with crypto-asset activities. Until recently, many of these activities were mainly performed by a small set of banks, some of which reportedly specialize in providing services to crypto-asset entities. More recently, a limited number of banks, including regional banks, custody banks, and the largest banks, announced plans to offer some of these services as well.

These activities may expose banks to some volatility in earnings as the volume of demand for these services fluctuates, especially if those banks are relatively specialized in providing services to crypto-asset entities. Connections to the crypto-asset ecosystem might also create some liquidity risks associated with providing deposit services to crypto-asset businesses. Banks could also face legal or reputational risk by association with developments in crypto-asset markets.

Banking organizations may also increase exposures to crypto-asset markets through lending activity. Loans secured by crypto-assets may result in crypto-assets temporarily coming on-balance sheet through debt previously contracted (DPC) authority. Overall, though, exposures to crypto-assets on bank balance sheets still

---

22 "Silvergate Purchases Blockchain Payment Network Assets from Diem," Silvergate, January 31, 2022, at https://ir.silvergate.com/news/news-details/2022/Silvergate-Purchases-Blockchain-Payment-Network-Assets-from-Diem/default.aspx.

23 "USDF Consortium™ Launches to Enable Banks to Mint USDF Stablecoins," Cision PR Newswire, Jan. 12, 2022, at https://www.prnewswire.com/news-releases/usdf-consortium-launches-to-enable-banks-to-mint-usdf-stablecoins-301458911.html. "Introducing the USDF Consortium™," USDF Consortium, 2022, at https://www.usdfconsortium.com/.

appear to be very limited.[24] Current interconnections are unlikely to cause banks to bear losses in response to a shock in the crypto-asset ecosystem. However, small exposures have the potential to grow rapidly.

In terms of scalability, some banks have indicated publicly that they have interest in offering crypto-asset products and services but are waiting on regulatory clarity before doing so. In addition, several third-party service providers or other firms could partner or collaborate with banking organizations. For example, a U.S.-based technology and financial services firm has announced that it offers banks and other financial institutions a platform that provides customers an access point to buy or sell Bitcoin, with the third party providing custody and execution.[25] Third parties of this kind create potential on-ramps for financial institutions to obtain greater scale of crypto-asset activities at a rapid pace. To date, very few banks have engaged in such activities. If banks were to scale up their participation in the crypto-asset ecosystem, such activity could potentially entail much greater access to the crypto-asset market by a broad range of institutional investors, corporations, and retail customers than currently exists.

Finally, crypto-asset entities continue to express interest in operating chartered banks at the state and federal levels. Such activities create another set of interconnections with the traditional financial system.

Publicly Offered Investment Products

A growing assortment of publicly offered financial products traded in regulated financial markets provides opportunities for rapid scaling of interconnections between participants in those markets and crypto-asset products. Aside from direct purchases of Bitcoin or other crypto-assets, investors can gain financial risk exposure to Bitcoin through publicly offered Bitcoin and Ether futures, swaps, and options on futures. Those instruments are also traded by additional products available to investors, including ETPs or mutual funds. Interconnections from these products extend to clearinghouses, regulated through the traditional financial system, which clear crypto-asset derivatives alongside more traditional derivatives products, indirectly exposing clearing members to risks associated with crypto-assets.

Investors may also hold shares in trusts that hold a pool of crypto-assets such as Bitcoin, Ethereum, and others. Investors can gain somewhat more indirect exposure

---

24   From an accounting perspective, banking organizations that custody crypto-assets on behalf of customers may have to reflect exposures on their balance sheet, as per SAB 121. This accounting would reflect a safeguarding liability and an associated asset, rather than showing the crypto-asset directly.

25   AnTy, "NYDIG to Offer Bitcoin Services to 70% of US Banks. NCR Partnership to Allow Exposure to 24M Customers," *Bitcoin Exchange Guide*, June 30, 2021, at https://bitcoinexchangeguide.com/nydig-to-offer-bitcoin-services-to-70-of-us-banks-ncr-partnership-to-allow-exposure-to-24m-customers/. NYDIG Bitcoin ETF, Form S-1 (February 16, 2021), at https://www.sec.gov/Archives/edgar/data/0001843021/000119312521043521/d242572ds1.htm.

to crypto-asset developments by purchasing equity of publicly traded companies that are focused on crypto-asset activities such as mining or operating crypto-asset platforms. A small but growing number of publicly traded companies hold crypto-assets in their corporate treasuries. Investors can also gain exposure to such companies through an ETP that tracks these companies or tracks an index such as the Nasdaq Blockchain Economy Index, which is made up of firms that support or utilize blockchain technology. Finally, a limited number of public companies have issued securities in crypto-asset form, i.e., tokenized shares that are issued and transferred using DLT. Tokenization of this kind may raise associated legal issues.

Private Investments

A growing set of private investments in crypto-asset entities and activities have been made by firms that are also permitted to hold other risky assets, including asset managers, hedge funds, venture capital funds, private funds, family offices, private corporations, and others. Some financial institutions may privately offer structured products with returns based on crypto-assets. These private investment products permit investments in practically all types of firms operating inside the crypto-asset ecosystem, including major crypto-asset platforms, blockchain service providers, miners, and other blockchain-related companies. Indeed, while some crypto-asset companies are publicly listed, many more are privately held and have received rounds of funding from venture capital funds, hedge funds, and others. Therefore, these investments provide direct exposure to losses on these investments and crypto-asset developments more broadly. In turn, these investment managers offer on-ramps to institutional investors to gain exposure to crypto-assets.

Industry surveys suggest that the scale of these investments grew quickly during the boom in crypto-asset markets through late 2021. In June 2022, PwC estimated that the number of crypto-specialist hedge funds was more than 300 globally, with $4.1 billion in assets under management. In addition, in a survey, PwC found that 38 percent of surveyed traditional hedge funds were currently investing in "digital assets," compared to 21 percent the year prior. However, many had relatively small investments of this kind.[26] Finally, start-ups in the crypto-asset ecosystem reportedly raised $25 billion in venture capital dollars in 2021, an eightfold increase from the prior year.[27]

While significant numbers of hedge funds or venture capital funds have some exposure to crypto-assets, most of these exposures are likely still small. For example, in a data set of crypto-asset holdings by more than 1,500 venture capital funds,

---

26   PwC Global Crypto Hedge Fund Report 2022, at https://www.pwc.com/gx/en/news-room/press-releases/2022/pwc-global-crypto-hedge-fund-report-2022.html.

27   "State of Blockchain 2021 Report," CBInsights, February 1, 2022, at https://www.cbinsights.com/research/report/blockchain-trends-2021/.

hedge funds, and other similar entities, only about fifteen had $1 billion or more investments as of July 2022.[28]

Interconnections with the traditional financial system through these types of investments are characterized by a large degree of opacity and may be complex.

Finally, some high-frequency trading firms are reportedly active in crypto-asset markets.[29] This activity exposes trading firms to potential losses from crypto-assets. For example, a high-frequency trading firm restored $320 million to compensate investors following the hack of and theft of assets from the Wormhole cross-chain bridge, illustrating the risks to firms and investors posed by interconnections with the crypto-asset ecosystem.[30]

On-ramps for Consumers and Retail Investors

Consumers and retail investors have many options for gaining exposure to crypto-assets.

Consumers and retail investors appear to largely interact with crypto-assets outside of the traditional financial system through crypto-asset platforms. Risks to consumers and retail investors may arise from the offering of products that could be securities, commodities, or derivatives if they are not offered in compliance with applicable law. Consumers and investors can also make purchases of crypto-assets from "Bitcoin ATM" kiosks or directly from other crypto holders through un-hosted wallets.

In the traditional financial system, consumers and retail investors can purchase publicly offered financial products related to crypto-assets. It is also possible for many American consumers to buy, sell, and hold crypto-assets through firms that provide other financial services, such as money services, payments, or broker-dealer services. For example, third parties that integrate the ability to buy and sell crypto-assets in banks' and credit unions' online services offer one on-ramp for consumer access to crypto-assets. As part of these retail on-ramps, these third parties may also offer back-end payment, clearing, and settlement services to financial institutions.

Credit, debit, and pre-paid cards offer consumers some services related to crypto-assets, including earning rewards denominated in crypto-assets and affiliations with crypto-asset entities that offer rewards which may vary based on the amount of crypto-assets held with those entities.

---

28   Analysis based on data collected by Autonomous Next (as of July 8, 2022).

29   Alexander Osipovich, "Big Bitcoin Exchange Welcomes High-Speed Traders," *The Wall Street Journal*, May 15, 2018, at https://www.wsj.com/articles/big-bitcoin-exchange-welcomes-high-speed-traders-1526385600.

30   Tom Wilson and Pushkala Aripaka, "Jump Trading replaces stolen Wormhole funds after $320 mln crypto hack," *Reuters*, February 3, 2022, at https://www.reuters.com/technology/crypto-network-wormhole-hit-with-possible-320-mln-hack-2022-02-03/.

Finally, retail investors have opportunities to invest in crypto-assets through retirement plans that have recently added such assets as investment options, or investors may have exposures to crypto-assets through their pension plans.[31]

The Federal Reserve's Survey of Household Economic Decisionmaking (SHED) found that 12 percent of adults used or held crypto-assets in the past year.[32] Other surveys have found somewhat higher figures, including 16 percent according to The Pew Research Center and 20 percent according to an NBC news poll.[33] Surveys have also found that racial minorities are relatively more likely to gravitate toward Bitcoin and other crypto-assets.[34] In January 2022, a survey of over 600 investment advisors found nearly all advisors had received inquiries about crypto-assets from investors in 2021 and that 15 percent allocated funds to crypto-assets in client accounts during the year, up from 6 percent in the prior year.[35]

Insurance Companies

A handful of U.S. insurance companies have reported holdings of crypto-assets. One survey of insurers found that 92 percent of respondent companies do not invest in crypto-assets.[36] Five companies reported exposure to crypto-assets with a total book/adjusted carrying value (BACV) of $188 million as of year-end 2020.[37] The majority of these holdings were acquired near the end of 2020. Compared to roughly $7 trillion of industry invested assets, crypto-assets holdings appear small.

---

31 US Department of Labor, "401(k) Plan Investments in 'Cryptocurrencies,'" March 10, 2022, at https://www.dol.gov/agencies/ebsa/employers-and-advisers/plan-administration-and-compliance/compliance-assistance-releases/2022-01.

32 Board of Governors of the Federal Reserve System, Economic Well-Being of U.S. Households in 2021, at https://www.federalreserve.gov/publications/files/2021-report-economic-well-being-us-households-202205.pdf.

33 Thomas Franck, "One in five adults has invested in, traded or used cryptocurrency, NBC News poll shows," *CNBC*, March 31, 2022, at https://www.cnbc.com/2022/03/31/cryptocurrency-news-21percent-of-adults-have-traded-or-used-crypto-nbc-poll-shows.html. Andrew Perrin, "16% of Americans say they have ever invested in, traded or used cryptocurrency," *Pew Research Center*, November 11, 2021, at https://www.pewresearch.org/fact-tank/2021/11/11/16-of-americans-say-they-have-ever-invested-in-traded-or-used-cryptocurrency/.

34 For more discussion, see United States Department of the Treasury, *Crypto-Assets: Implications for Consumers, Investors, and Businesses*, September 2022, at https://home.treasury.gov/system/files/136/CryptoAsset_EO5.pdf.

35 "94% of Advisors Received Questions About Crypto From Clients in 2021, Bitwise/ETF Trends Survey Finds," January 20, 2022, at https://bitwiseinvestments.com/crypto-market-insights/94-percent-of-advisors-received-questions-about-crypto-from-clients-in-2021-bitwise-etf-trends-survey-finds.

36 "Insurance Survey 2022," Goldman Sachs Insurance Asset Management, at https://www.gsam.com/content/gsam/us/en/institutions/market-insights/gsam-insights/2022/Insurance_Survey_2022.html.

37 According to filings of Schedule BA and Schedule D Part 2 Section 2 (Common Stocks)

Prospectively, another channel for interconnections may be insurance policies held by crypto-asset firms, either for cybersecurity risks or other policies such as coverage of digital wallets.[38]

Other Potential Interconnections with the Traditional Financial System

Some municipalities have announced their intentions to accept crypto-assets for payments, including tax payments, although the scale of adoption by taxpayers appears to be very limited to date.[39] Given the volatility of crypto-asset prices, such asset holdings may introduce financial risk to these municipalities who would need to convert these assets to dollars to make payments on obligations, which may include debt obligations held by traditional financial institutions. In addition, some nonfinancial corporations accept crypto-assets for payments and hold crypto-assets in their corporate treasuries. Such activities may also increase credit risk elsewhere in the traditional financial system, for example, if banks make loans to municipalities that are exposed to crypto-asset price volatility.

Some mortgage finance companies have originated mortgages collateralized by crypto-assets and have announced plans to potentially pool these mortgages together to offer to investors as bonds in a securitization format.[40] Overall, the scale of this activity appears to be very small to date. In addition, some traditional mortgage lenders have reportedly explored ways to integrate crypto-assets into the mortgage business. For example, one mortgage company launched a temporary pilot program that accepted crypto-assets for mortgage payments, but ultimately discontinued the program.[41] Such connections could potentially impact household financial conditions if homeowners' ability to comply with the terms of their mortgage contracts is affected by the volatility of crypto-asset prices.

Finally, correlations of crypto-asset prices with prices of risky assets in the traditional financial system give a general indication of interconnections. These correlations may arise if through common exposure to macroeconomic or financial developments, or through the risk premia of market participants that operate in both markets. Correlations between crypto-assets such as spot Bitcoin prices

---

38 Ian Allison, "Lloyd's-Licensed Broker Launches Crypto Insurance Product," *CoinDesk*, May 11, 2022, at https://www.coindesk.com/business/2022/05/11/lloyds-licensed-broker-launches-crypto-insurance-product/.

39 Michael Bologna, "Crypto Crash Halts Plans by Statehouses to Accept Bitcoin Tax Payments," *Bloomberg*, July 5, 2022, at https://www.bloomberg.com/news/articles/2022-07-05/crypto-crash-weighs-on-states-plans-for-tax-payment-by-bitcoin.

40 Heather Perlberg, "Crypto Mortgages Let Homebuyers Keep Bitcoin, Put Nothing Down," *Bloomberg*, April 27, 2022, at https://www.bloomberg.com/news/articles/2022-04-27/buying-real-estate-with-crypto-new-mortgages-are-backed-by-coins.

41 MacKenzie Sigalos, "Second-largest U.S. mortgage lender ditches its plan to accept payments in bitcoin," *CNBC*, October 14, 2021, at https://www.cnbc.com/2021/10/14/united-wholesale-mortgage-ditches-its-plan-to-accept-bitcoin-ethereum.html.

and risky traditional assets such as broad equity indexes have generally been high though somewhat volatile, as shown in **Figure 3**. Rather than providing a source of potentially diversified investments, crypto-assets are increasingly priced in ways that appear to be broadly linked with traditional risky financial asset developments. In some instances, large crypto-asset price movements have coincided with similar movements in the prices of other risky financial assets.

Figure 3: Correlations between Bitcoin Prices and Equity Prices

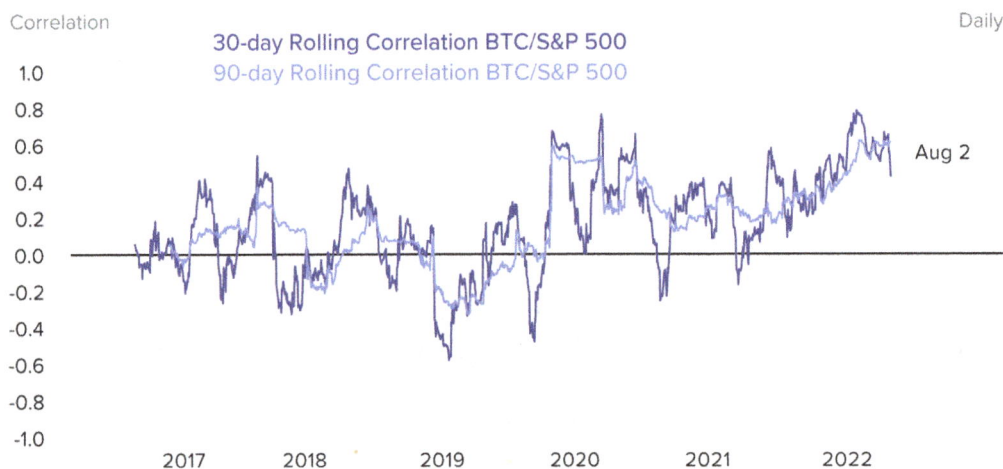

Source: CryptoCompare

3.3 Vulnerabilities Inside the Crypto-Asset Ecosystem

3.3.1 Crypto-Asset Prices

Crypto-asset prices appear to be based largely on speculation and not anchored by clear fundamental current economic uses. In addition, prices may be affected by the prevalence of fraud and market manipulation.

As a result, crypto-asset markets are subject to the risk that a shock could induce significant drops in prices. For example, malicious attacks that steal crypto-assets may put significant downward pressure on asset prices, partly by lowering market sentiment. Indeed, reports have suggested that an attack on the now defunct crypto-asset platform Mt. Gox led to a widespread decline in market sentiment and crypto-asset prices in 2013.[42]

---

42   Andy Greenberg, "Bitcoin's Price Plummets as Mt. Gox Goes Dark, with Massive Hack Rumored," *Forbes*, February 25, 2014, at https://www.forbes.com/sites/andygreenberg/2014/02/25/bitcoins-price-plummets-as-mt-gox-goes-dark-with-massive-hack-rumored/?sh=53a40683ce1f.

Market participants that hold crypto-assets on their balance sheets are particularly exposed to potential market losses on those assets in response to a shock. Retail participation directly exposes Americans to losses on crypto-asset holdings when asset prices fall. According to Pew Research Center, among those who said they held crypto-assets, 46 percent reported their investments did worse than they expected, versus only 15 percent who reported better-than-expected results.[43]

In general, whether potential price declines represent financial stability risk is difficult to determine in isolation but should be considered in conjunction with other vulnerabilities. When combined with leverage or funding mismatches, market losses can lead to material risks to financial stability. For example, price declines could expose leveraged positions, potentially leading to deleveraging or liquidation and causing further price declines. Price declines could also cause investors to reassess the safety of their investments and seek withdrawal of invested funds, for example at crypto-asset platforms, potentially putting stress on institutions with funding mismatches.

As an illustration of the financial stability implications of significant asset price declines, the substantial decline in crypto-asset prices during late 2021 and early 2022 reportedly coincided with some key market developments. First, many crypto-asset proponents have forecasted that crypto-asset prices would continue to grow significantly over a long period, though they may have had financial incentives to make such forecasts. The investment strategy of the highly interconnected hedge fund Three Arrows Capital was reportedly partly informed by a speculative "supercycle" theory of crypto-asset prices along these lines.[44] Box B discusses how the failure of Three Arrows Capital in more detail. Second, commentators have noted the possibility that the purported liquidation of the Luna Foundation Guard's Bitcoin holdings, if it occurred, could have put procyclical downward pressure on Bitcoin prices[45] and on crypto-asset market sentiment more broadly, as discussed in Box C which describes the collapse of the TerraUSD stablecoin.[46]

---

43 Michelle Faverio and Navid Massarat, "46% of Americans who have invested in cryptocurrency say it's done worse than expected," Pew Research, August 23, 2022, at https://www.pewresearch.org/fact-tank/2022/08/23/46-of-americans-who-have-invested-in-cryptocurrency-say-its-done-worse-than-expected/.

44 Justina Lee, Muyao Shen, and Ben Bartenstein, "How Three Arrows Capital Blew Up and Set Off a Crypto Contagion," *Bloomberg*, July 12, 2022, at https://www.bloomberg.com/news/features/2022-07-13/how-crypto-hedge-fund-three-arrows-capital-fell-apart-3ac.

45 Matt Levine, "Terra Flops," *Bloomberg*, May 11, 2022, at https://www.bloomberg.com/opinion/articles/2022-05-11/terra-flops. Jacquelyn Melinek, "Bitcoin's value nears $30,000 mark as Luna Foundation Guard liquidates wallet," *TechCrunch*, May 9, 2022, at https://techcrunch.com/2022/05/09/bitcoins-value-nears-30000-mark-as-luna-foundation-guard-liquidates-wallet/.

46 David Yaffe-Bellany and Erin Griffith, "How a Trash-Talking Crypto Founder Caused a $40 Billion Crash," *The New York Times*, May 18, 2022, at https://www.nytimes.com/2022/05/18/technology/terra-luna-cryptocurrency-do-kwon.html.

Crypto-Asset Price Volatility

Crypto-asset prices have been very volatile and prone to both substantial gains and substantial drops. For example, the realized volatility of spot Bitcoin prices has been higher than the realized volatility of traditional assets such as oil, equities, or bonds, as shown in **Figure 4**. This figure includes data from 2018 through July 31, 2022, which includes a substantial runup in crypto prices starting in late 2020 and a substantial decline over the first half of 2022. Notably, declines in crypto-asset prices include a broad-based decline in 2018, when, for example, the price of Bitcoin fell about 80 percent over the course of the year. In addition, crypto-asset prices declined broadly in late 2021 and early 2022, when, for example, the price of Bitcoin fell about 75 percent over seven months. In these episodes, crypto-asset prices have tended to be widely correlated with each other, exposing crypto-asset market participants to largely non-diversifiable risk inside the crypto-asset ecosystem.

Figure 4: Annualized Realized Price Volatility of Crypto-Assets and Traditional Assets

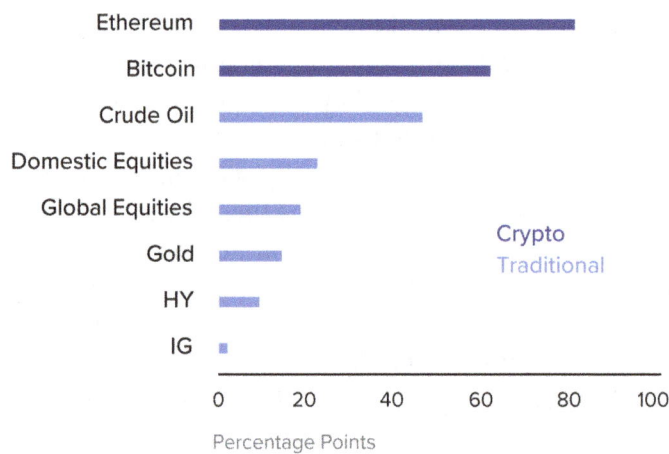

Note: Data are from 2018 to July 31, 2022. Source: Staff calculations; Bloomberg Finance L.P.

Lack of Clear Fundamental Economic Uses to Anchor Prices

Fundamental economic use cases do not currently anchor prices of many crypto-assets. Rather than reflecting analysis of cash flows, crypto-asset prices may reflect the probability that economic use cases could develop in the future, balanced against the probability, as expressed by some industry commenters, that no significant economic uses for blockchain technologies may develop.[47]

---

47 *See* "Letter in Support of Responsible Fintech Policy," from 1500 computer scientists, software engineers, and technologists, at https://concerned.tech/.

Supporting this premise, the financial press commonly reports so-called "technical" or "chartist" analysis for crypto-asset prices, which emphasizes psychological factors and does not involve any analysis of fundamental economic factors.[48] Chartist analysis is not unique to crypto-asset markets but may garner more attention in those markets because of the outsized importance of sentiment and psychological factors.

The market for crypto-assets known as "non-fungible tokens" (NFTs) also illustrates concerns about the lack of fundamental economic use cases. Most, if not all, NFTs strike many observers as having little to no real value, though NFT proponents have debated this point and emphasized commonalities with the art market or uses in video games.[49] Even given that the value of an NFT may be tied to a digital good or collectible, the market for NFTs has exhibited the classic characteristics of an investment mania and bubble. Indeed, by the summer of 2022, the volume of NFT transactions had fallen substantially after growing tremendously over the previous year, as shown in **Figure 5**.[50] Though it is difficult to track NFT prices over time, prices appear to have fallen substantially in 2022, roughly tracking the overall decline in crypto-asset prices.

---

48 "Bitcoin's plummet has pushed it through just about every recent technical support level, forcing traders to now consider $30,000 as the next line in the sand." Vildana Hajric and Akayla Gardner, "Bitcoins New Floor is $30,000 as 50% Rout Destroys Old Supports," *Bloomberg*, January 24, 2022, at https://www.bloomberg.com/news/articles/2022-01-24/-30-000-is-bitcoin-s-new-floor-as-50-rout-destroys-old-supports. Joshua Oliver, "Bitcoin drops below key $20,000 threshold," *Financial Times*, June 19, 2022, at https://www.ft.com/content/97b5a774-d817-4d3b-82b2-6bbe22c3d59b.

49 Kevin Roose, "What are NFTs?" *The New York Times*, March 18, 2022, at https://www.nytimes.com/interactive/2022/03/18/technology/nft-guide.html.

50 Scott Reyburn, "Art's NFT Question: Next Frontier in Trading, or a New Form of Tulip?" *The New York Times*, March 30, 2021, at https://www.nytimes.com/2021/03/30/arts/design/nft-bubble.html.

Figure 5: Reported Trading Volume of NFTs

Millions of Dollars   Monthly

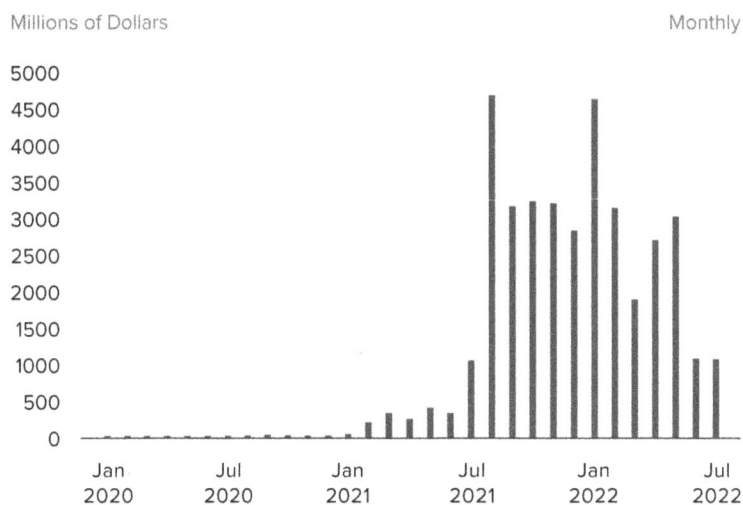

Source: Nonfungible.com

In addition to the absence of strong fundamental economic use cases to date, crypto-assets also do not have an extensive price history that can provide much guidance on whether current prices are high relative to some historic statistical average. Though Bitcoin has traded for over a decade, the early price history does not provide much guidance on whether current prices are prone to outsized drops.

Currently, disclosures made by crypto-asset promoters may have limited use in informing asset prices. Crypto-asset projects are typically promoted through "white papers" and social media. Those communications may be unclear or more technically complex than an average investor may be able to fully understand. In other cases, "white papers" may be little more than a few pages of graphics and some promotional language. General promotional materials may also lack information that is commonly relied upon for valuing investments, such as the rights of holders and obligations of issuers, information about the management team, a project plan or timeline, financial statements, or disclosures about funding sources. Crypto-asset promotional communications may contain misleading or false statements or omissions. Materials made available by crypto-asset promoters may also lack uniformity in how information is presented, limiting users' ability to compare one crypto-asset with another.

Speculation

As a result of a lack of fundamental economic use cases, crypto-asset prices appear to be driven in large part by sentiment and future expectations. Speculation is a common motivation for participation in crypto-asset markets. Speculators by their nature do not seek to hold assets for a specific economic purpose but rather to gain exposure to potential price swings.

Financial history provides famous examples of a large volume of speculative activity driving asset prices to extremely high levels, thereby leaving prices vulnerable to substantial declines. Of course, speculation has often been motivated by major economic developments, such as significant financial innovations, and those innovations likely would have driven up asset prices even without a large degree of speculative activity.

Survey data provides some limited evidence on the prevalence of speculation in crypto-asset markets. The Federal Reserve's 2022 SHED found that more than 90 percent of adults who had used or held crypto-assets in the past year had held them for investment purposes rather than for payments, although not all investment purposes necessarily involve speculation.[51]

The large presence of speculation may suggest that price volatility among crypto-assets is a feature market participants deliberately seek out. Many market participants may have trading strategies that are predicated on high volatility, a portfolio strategy that includes an allocation to high volatility assets, or are simply attracted by casino-like elements. The major rise in crypto-asset market capitalization in 2020 and 2021 came amidst a broader rise in gamification of retail participation in financial markets, for example, by "YOLOing the market."[52] Such activities may combine gaming, social interaction, entertainment, and wider cultural trends. Participants use many popular terms in crypto-asset markets to highlight the emphasis on speculation. For example, guides have increasingly circulated online about making money by trading in so-called "meme coins" or "hype coins," among certain other terms, i.e., assets that have no apparent utility beyond speculative hype or jokes.[53] So-called gamification of crypto-asset markets may facilitate the entrance of retail participants who would not usually participate in equity and fixed income markets and who may not be attuned to the importance of disclosures and investor protection rules.[54] These factors make the market ripe for fraud, self-dealing, insider trading, and other market misconduct, as discussed next.

---

51   Board of Governors of the Federal Reserve System, *Economic Well-Being of U.S. Households in 2021*, May 2022, https://www.federalreserve.gov/publications/files/2021-report-economic-well-being-us-households-202205.pdf.

52   Maggie Sklar, "'YOLOing the Market': Market Manipulation? Implications for Markets and Financial Stability." March 2021, at https://www.chicagofed.org/-/media/publications/policy-discussion-papers/2021/pdp-2021-01-pdf.pdf?sc_lang=en.

53   David Segal, "Going for Broke in Cryptoland," *The New York Times*, August 5, 2021, at https://www.nytimes.com/2021/08/05/business/hype-coins-cryptocurrency.html.

54   "Blockchain and Gamification – A Match Made in Heaven" *Bitcoinist*, at https://bitcoinist.com/blockchain-gamification-match-made-heaven/.

Fraud and Manipulation

Fraud and market manipulation are a third factor shaping crypto-asset prices. There have been many instances of fraud and market manipulation in crypto-asset markets. Such schemes often can have the effect of artificially inflating the price of specific crypto-assets temporarily and undermining confidence in the integrity of any given price. Indeed, market participants may misinterpret the effects of fraudulent or manipulative activity, such as rising prices and increasing trading volume, as indicating a greater level of investor interest than actually exists. More generally, the unraveling of fraudulent schemes may involve substantial and sudden declines in asset prices.

For example, in the spot Bitcoin market, the SEC has identified possible sources of fraud and manipulation, taking several forms, including "wash" trading for example.[55] While it is likely very difficult to measure the full extent of fraudulent activity, **Figure 6** shows one measure of the estimated extent of financial scams and "rug pulls" during the past six years, globally.[56]

Figure 6: Estimated Volume of Crypto-Asset-Related Scams

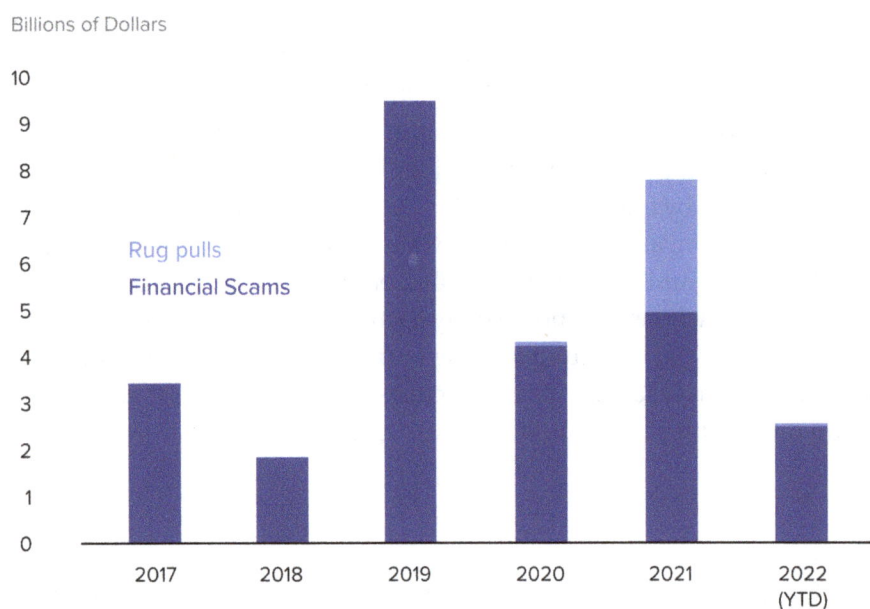

Source: Chainalysis. Data for 2022 include up to July 31, 2022.

---

55   SEC, Release No. 34-95180, June 29, 2022, at https://www.sec.gov/rules/sro/nysearca/2022/34-95180.pdf.

56   For more details on the estimated volume of scams, see Chainalysis, "The Biggest Threat to Trust in Cryptocurrency: Rug Pulls Put 2021 Cryptocurrency Scam Revenue Close to All-time Highs" December 16, 2021, at https://blog.chainalysis.com/reports/2021-crypto-scam-revenues/.

The volume of complaints from members of the public may give some indication of fraudulent activity in crypto-asset markets, in addition to other potential sources of complaints such as operational disruptions. Such complaints might be expected to increase with the overall increase in the scale of the market. The SEC has received over 23,000 tips, complaints, and referrals since fiscal year 2019 involving crypto-asset activities, as shown in **Figure 7**. Common subjects of these reports to the SEC include initial "coin" or "token" offerings, crypto-asset wallet access issues, crypto-asset platform operational issues, pricing and manipulation, and high-yield investment schemes that purport to involve crypto-asset trading and mining.

Figure 7: Tips, Complaints, and Referrals Received by the SEC Related to Crypto-Asset Activities

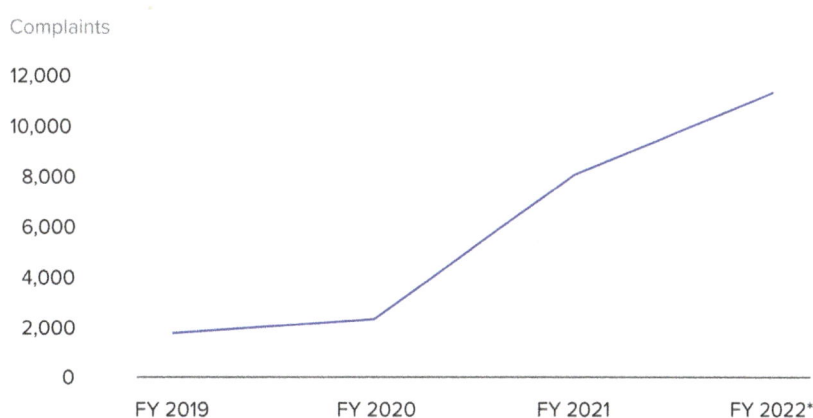

Source: SEC. Data for fiscal year 2022 (which ends September 30) are through July 31, 2022

Complaints filed with the CFPB regarding crypto-assets show a similar sharp increase over the past couple of years, as shown in **Figure 8**.[57] In addition, reports in the Sentinel database maintained by the Federal Trade Commission (FTC)—which contains reports filed directly with the FTC in addition to reports from other sources such as those filed with the CFPB—also show a large recent increase, as shown in **Figure 9**. One common subject of the Sentinel reports is fraud via an investment scam, and the median individual reported loss is $2,600.[58]

---

57 Data on complaints submitted to the CFPB is current as of August 1, 2022 and excludes some complaints (e.g., multiple complaints submitted by a given consumer on the same issue, whistleblower tips, and complaints that the Bureau found were not actionable).

58 *See* Emma Fletcher, "Reports Show Scammers Cashing in on Crypto Craze," Federal Trade Commission, June 3, 2022, at https://www.ftc.gov/news-events/data-visualizations/data-spotlight/2022/06/reports-show-scammers-cashing-crypto-craze. The other numbers reported on that website related to the volume of complaints differ somewhat from the numbers reported here, which include not just reports made directly to the FTC but reports collected from other sources as well through the FTC's Sentinel database.

Figure 8: Complaints Submitted to the CFPB Related to Crypto-Asset Activities

Complaints

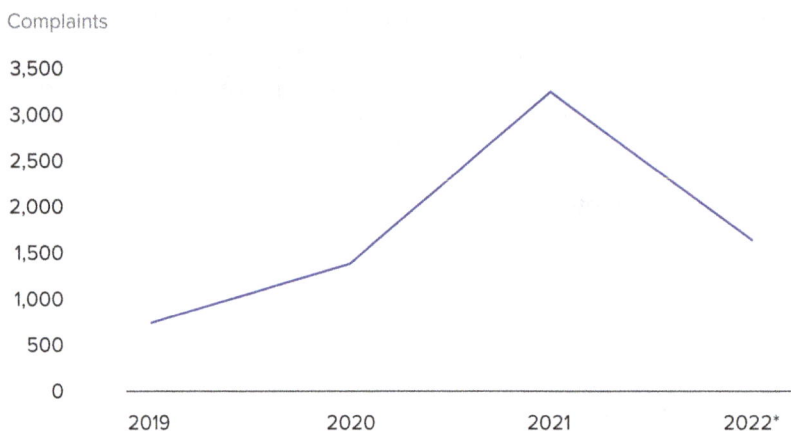

Source: CFPB. Data for the calendar year 2022 are through July 31, 2022. For this chart, crypto-asset complaints refer to complaints submitted to the CFPB in which consumers selected the sub-product "virtual currency" as the subject of the complaint.

Figure 9: Reports in the FTC Sentinel Database Related to Crypto-Asset Activities

Complaints

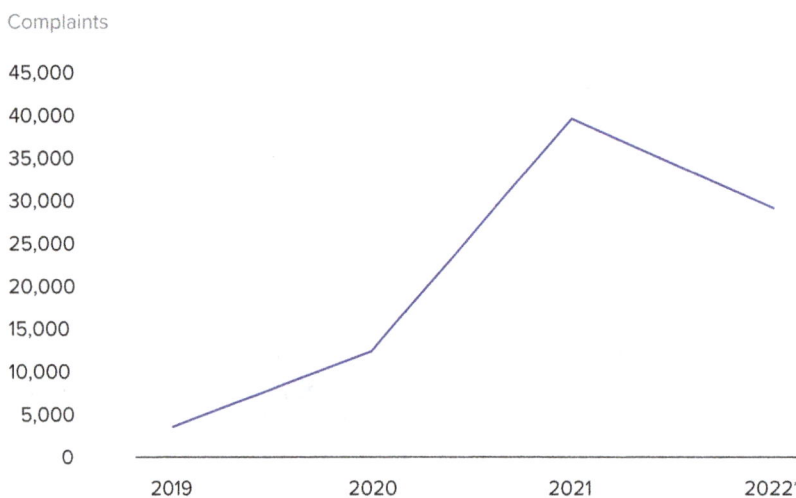

Source: FTC. Data for calendar year 2022 are through July 31, 2022.

Regulators have brought charges against participants in numerous types of fraudulent schemes, which may inflate asset prices for a time. One type of scam is a Ponzi scheme, in which the payment of purported returns to existing investors is made from funds contributed by new investors. In many such schemes, rather than engaging in any legitimate investment activity, the fraudulent actors focus on attracting new money to make promised payments to earlier investors and diverting some of these "invested" funds for personal use. Ponzi schemes may inflate asset prices by drawing general investor interest to crypto-assets. In 2013, the SEC charged that the Bitcoin Savings and Trust was a Ponzi scheme that promised 7 percent weekly returns to investors but actually paid out these profits using inflows of new investment funds. The scheme raised $4.5 million.[59] The SEC's Office of Investor Education and Advocacy has issued an alert to warn individual investors about Ponzi schemes.[60] In 2022, the CFTC charged that products offered through the websites Empowercoin, Ecoinplus, and JetCoin were Ponzi schemes that promised daily profits and together attracted $44 million of investment funds.[61] The SEC has also filed complaints regarding alleged pyramid schemes.[62]

"Rug pulls" are a type of exit scam that may trigger the collapse of a crypto-asset's price after a period of inflation.[63] Prior to a rug pull, developers or others promote a crypto-asset project, which may have the false appearance of being a legitimate project. Later, scammers abscond with any funds provided by investors. **Figure 6** shows that rug pulls have reportedly proliferated recently, as scammers have preyed on growing investor interest. Rug pulls may involve scammers creating and contributing to a liquidity pool in a DeFi protocol in the form of a new crypto-asset, often a stablecoin. One form of a rug pull is executed when, after a period of promotion and attraction of investors, the crypto-asset creator withdraws all of their own contributions from the liquidity pool abruptly, causing the price of the new crypto-asset to crash. Rug pulls may also involve covert restrictions on sell orders. For example, the Squid Game crypto-asset scam stole over $3 million from investors, partly because they were unaware of restrictions on their ability to sell the crypto-asset.[64] Finally, rug pulls may also involve the coding of an explicit, malicious back-door into a new crypto-asset smart contract, which allows the developer to pull out all the liquidity of the crypto-asset at once.[65]

59   SEC, "SEC Charges Texas Man With Running Bitcoin-Denominated Ponzi Scheme," July 23, 2013, at https://www.sec.gov/news/press-release/2013-132.

60   SEC Office of Investor Education and Advocacy, "Ponzi Schemes Using Virtual Currencies," at https://www.sec.gov/files/ia_virtualcurrencies.pdf.

61   CFTC, "CFTC Charges Four Operators for $44 Million Bitcoin Ponzi and Misappropriation Schemes," March 8, 2022, at https://www.cftc.gov/PressRoom/PressReleases/8498-22.

62   SEC, "SEC Sues Alleged Perpetrator of Fraudulent Pyramid Scheme Promising Investors Cryptocurrency Riches," May 23, 2109, at https://www.sec.gov/news/press-release/2019-74.

63   CFTC, "Customer Advisory: Beware Virtual Currency Pump-and-Dump Schemes," at https://www.cftc.gov/sites/default/files/2019-12/customeradvisory_pumpdump0218.pdf.

64   Chris Stokel-Walker, "How a Squid Game Crypto Scam Got Away With Millions," Wired, November 2, 2021, at https://www.wired.com/story/squid-game-coin-crypto-scam/.

65   Valerio Puggini, "Crypto rug pulls: what is a rug pull in crypto and 6 ways to spot it," Coin Telegraph, February 6, 2022, at https://cointelegraph.com/explained/crypto-rug-pulls-what-is-a-rug-pull-in-crypto-and-6-ways-to-spot-it. And, Koinly, "Rug Pulls: Your Complete Guide," March 31, 2022, at https://koinly.io/blog/crypto-rug-pulls-guide/.

Simple pump-and-dump schemes may have similar effects. For example, in 2021, the CFTC charged two individuals with scamming investors for a total of $2 million through a pump-and-dump scheme in which they promoted crypto-assets through social media as valuable long-term investments, and then sold their holdings as prices rose sharply following those deceptive endorsements.[66]

Market participants may inflate asset prices through other manipulative actions. For example, wash trading may create the appearance of higher activity and liquidity than actually exists, attracting investors under false pretenses. Platforms may have economic incentives to create such false pretenses, and such incentives are harder to constrain if market participants are acting outside of, or in non-compliance with, laws and regulations. In 2021, the CFTC charged Coinbase with wash trading, finding that an employee used a manipulative or deceptive device by intentionally placing buy and sell orders in a trading pair of Bitcoin and Litecoin that matched each other as wash trades.[67] This created the misleading appearance of liquidity and trading interest in Litecoin.[68] In addition, in 2022, the Department of Justice and the SEC both took action against a former trading platform employee and others involved in an alleged insider trading scheme, alleging they profited from confidential information about which crypto-assets were scheduled to be listed on the platform.[69]

Crypto-asset proponents have argued that the transparent nature of transactions on permissionless blockchains could mitigate fraud and price manipulation. At the same time, the transparent nature of a blockchain appears to itself create opportunities for attacks or manipulation. For example, so-called "sandwich attacks" involve front-running publicly visible pending transactions.[70] Many commentators have also noted the ability of transaction validators to profit off of pending transactions, known as "miner extractable value."[71]

---

66 CFTC, "CFTC Charges Two Individuals with Multi-Million Dollar Digital Asset Pump-and-Dump Scheme," March 5, 2021, at https://www.cftc.gov/PressRoom/PressReleases/8366-21.

67 *See also CFTC v. Gemini Trust Co., LLC*, No. 22-cv-4563 (S.D.N.Y. filed June 2, 2022)

68 CFTC, "CFTC Orders Coinbase Inc. to Pay $6.5 Million for False, Misleading, or Inaccurate Reporting and Wash Trading," at https://www.cftc.gov/PressRoom/PressReleases/8369-21.

69 Department of Justice, "Three Charged in First Ever Cryptocurrency Insider Trading Tipping Scheme" July 21, 2022, at https://www.justice.gov/usao-sdny/pr/three-charged-first-ever-cryptocurrency-insider-trading-tipping-scheme.

70 Andrey Sergeenkov, "What Are Sandwich Attacks in DeFi and How Can You Avoid them?" CoinMarketCap, at https://coinmarketcap.com/alexandria/article/what-are-sandwich-attacks-in-defi-and-how-can-you-avoid-them.

71 Daian, Philip, et al. "Flash boys 2.0: Frontrunning in decentralized exchanges, miner extractable value, and consensus instability." *2020 IEEE Symposium on Security and Privacy (SP)*. IEEE, 2020, at https://par.nsf.gov/servlets/purl/10159474.

Liquidity Fragmentation

Finally, fragmentation of liquidity across multiple crypto-asset platforms and pools may make crypto-assets markets vulnerable to poor liquidity conditions and asset price dislocations. Faced with fragmented liquidity, crypto-asset holders wishing to exit their positions may have no choice but to sell crypto-assets at prices below those that would prevail given adequate liquidity, as discussed in part 3.3.5, Leverage. The reduced sales prices may push down asset prices even in crypto-asset platforms that do not have fragmented liquidity. In other cases, market participants may decide not to sell if the price required to execute a trade is higher than the projected proceeds of selling the crypto-assets. Additionally, liquidity fragmentation may occur when similar assets exist both on- and off-chain, such as when a firm issues a tokenized version of a traditional asset. Interoperability across crypto and non-crypto networks may exacerbate liquidity concerns in a particular type of issuance if market participants favor one type of asset over the other.

3.3.2 Financial Exposures via Interconnections within the Crypto-Asset Ecosystem

Interconnections inside the crypto-asset ecosystem spread losses if a shock causes the default of an interconnected entity and its counterparties then incur knock-on losses. Losses can also spread from common holdings if an entity holds a crypto-asset that records a sharp price decline. The crypto-asset ecosystem currently features a number of significantly interconnected entities, including crypto-asset platforms, investors, and other counterparties. The failure of a significantly interconnected entity can cause substantial distress within the crypto-asset ecosystem.

Platforms

In the crypto-asset ecosystem, major crypto-asset platforms offer an integrated suite of services and may have significant interconnections. Platforms may exacerbate the impact of interconnections compared to traditional financial institutions, such as banks, which are subject to macroprudential standards and prudential regulation and supervision, and may be beneficiaries of a public safety net. Integrated crypto-asset platforms often provide a range of services, including facilitating customers' trading in crypto-assets, custodying customer assets, maintaining order books, market making, and margin lending. Some crypto-asset platforms also issue stablecoins, offer high yields on invested funds, and engage in lending. Such platforms may have conflicts of interest due to their integrated structure.

Liquidity conditions in crypto-asset markets could deteriorate in response to the failure of a major crypto-asset platform, particularly in areas where that platform supports market trading and funding. Failure of a platform could lead to a downward liquidity spiral. When a crypto-asset platform acts as a sizable market maker or provides significant trading leverage to counterparties, its failure could have material impacts on the market. Such impacts could include abrupt reductions in liquidity, which could be especially acute if interoperability limitations across platforms force counterparties to exit leveraged positions. Impacts could also include increased trading spreads and collateral demands and possibly reduced customer confidence in crypto-asset firms' risk management practices and in crypto-assets themselves.

Short-term wholesale crypto-asset funding conditions could also deteriorate in response to a large crypto-asset platform's failure, if that platform acts as a conduit between crypto borrowers and lenders. Additional transaction complications could lead to substantial increases in lending rates, and lenders could fail to roll over loans, increase collateral requirements, or generally withdraw funding from credit markets as they seek alternative ways to continue or conclude their relationships. Altogether, in such a scenario, firms relying on short-term borrowing can fail rapidly after losing access to that funding.

Markets for crypto-assets affiliated with, or sponsored by, a platform may deteriorate if a platform were to fail. Crypto-asset platforms may currently have incentives to originate, distribute, and provide liquidity support for crypto-assets used on, or issued by, the crypto-asset platform itself, including but not limited to collateralized stablecoins. In response to a crypto-asset platform's failure, trading prices and collateral values for those assets may fall and holders of those assets may experience immediate capital losses.

More broadly, failure of a major crypto-asset platform would likely lead to losses for persons and businesses with which it transacts directly, i.e., customers and counterparties. Such a failure could also affect market participants' ability to sell and convert crypto-assets into national currency. For example, more than one million Celsius customers reportedly could not access their invested funds after it froze withdrawals.[72] Similarly, over one million Voyager customers were reportedly unable to access their invested funds after Voyager suspended withdrawals and subsequently filed for bankruptcy protection.[73] If crypto-asset activities were to scale up significantly, such disruptions could affect household and business spending. In particular, because there is no direct mechanism for customers to trade across different crypto-asset platforms, customers may be significantly locked into individual crypto-asset platforms during times of distress, unless they wish to

---

72 Vicky Ge Huang, "Big Crypto Lender Celsius Freezes All Account Withdrawals," *The Wall Street Journal*, June 13, 2022. https://www.wsj.com/articles/big-crypto-lender-celsius-freezes-all-account-withdrawals-11655096584.

73 Vicky Ge Huang, "Crypto Broker Voyager Digital Suspends Redemptions" *The Wall Street Journal* July 1, 2022, at https://www.wsj.com/articles/crypto-broker-voyager-digital-suspends-withdrawals-11656705822. And Voyager Digital, "Voyager Digital Reports Revenue of US$102.7 million for the quarter ended March 31, 2022," May 16, 2022 at https://www.prnewswire.com/news-releases/voyager-digital-reports-revenue-of-us102-7-million-for-the-quarter-ended-march-31--2022--301547719.html.

withdraw their assets directly into private wallets and as long as withdrawals are permitted and subject to transaction fees. Similar issues may apply to many of the most popular stablecoins, as some do not afford U.S. retail users any redemption rights, as noted in Box E.

Customers may have significant holdings at crypto-asset platforms based on the belief that the funds belong to them, not the crypto-asset platform, potentially leading to losses in excess of what customers can easily withstand. For example, in times of high price volatility, customers generally have a heightened interest in trading, but congestion tends to rise on blockchains and increased demand for transactions results in high fees. Retail customers seeking to quickly exit a crypto-asset platform may face the choice of remaining on the platform or incurring sizable fees, especially if users are either interacting directly with blockchains via self-hosted wallets or DeFi protocols, or if they are sending crypto-assets from one platform to another.[74]

In addition, platforms' practice of placing customers' crypto-assets into omnibus holding accounts, in which those assets are commingled with those of the platform, raises the risk that the bankruptcy of a platform could leave its customers as general creditors and vulnerable to losses or delays on their asset holdings. Bankruptcy courts might deem a platform's custodial holdings to be the property of the bankrupt platform, rather than of its customers.[75] At least one major crypto-asset platform has acknowledged that customer funds, which are commingled with the funds of the platform, may be considered the property of the bankruptcy estate in the event of insolvency.[76]

Finally, the failure of a large platform might also disrupt another platform through operational relationships or through other connections such as debt or equity investments. For example, as indicated by **Figure B-1** in Box B, some platforms made loans to other platforms that are now in bankruptcy, including Celsius and Voyager Digital.

The capital and liquidity buffers held by large crypto-asset platforms are key factors in considering their interconnection risks inside the crypto-asset ecosystem, though the vulnerabilities that platforms pose to the financial stability of the broader U.S. financial system would depend on additional factors including platforms' overall scale and interconnections with traditional financial institutions. Evaluating the adequacy of platforms' capital and liquidity buffers could be challenging given limited publicly available information about the structure of platform operations and risk management. Evaluation of the adequacy of these buffers would require

---

74   Blocknative, "Why are ETH Gas Fees So High?" August 3, 2022, at https://www.blocknative.com/blog/why-eth-gas-fees-high.

75   Adam Levitin, "Not Your Keys, Not Your Coins: Unpriced Credit Risk in Cryptocurrency," *Texas Law Review*, vol. 101, 2022. https://papers.ssrn.com/sol3/papers.cfm?abstract_id=4107019.

76   *See* Coinbase's 10-Q filing for March 31, 2022.

information on the risks that large crypto-asset platforms are exposed to, and risk management protocols. Capital and liquidity buffers could be limited. In the context of potential vertically integrated market structures, as discussed in more detail in part 5.3.3, Markets or Activities Featuring Direct Retail Access, the capital adequacy of large platforms takes on particularly large importance given the lack of intermediaries that may help absorb losses or limit risks to the clearinghouse. Crypto-asset market participants have argued that automated position liquidation can provide a first line of defense, placing less importance on capital buffers.[77]

"Whales"

Crypto-asset markets have shown clear risks can arise from concentrated exposures to single large counterparties or investors. For example, Box B describes the failure of Three Arrows Capital, and the fallout that commentators have ascribed to its many interconnections and large positions in crypto-asset markets. In general, large exposures have arisen repeatedly in crypto-asset markets in the absence of firms implementing adequate counterparty exposure limits. One study has found that the top 1,000 market participants owned roughly one-sixth of Bitcoin in circulation at the end of 2020, and the top 10,000 participants owned roughly one-third of Bitcoin in circulation at the time.[78] Large holders of this kind create the potential for significant interconnections, depending on their counterparties' sizes and exposure limits.

News media accounts include many reports of so-called "whales" that hold large positions relative to the size of their counterparties, such as trading, lending, or borrowing platforms. Those counterparties can come under financial pressure if these large exposures face losses or liquidation. For example, in October 2021, a single user reportedly withdrew over $4.2 billion in crypto-assets from a DeFi liquidity protocol, causing lending and borrowing interest rates on the protocol to spike and leading to an 18 percent decline of total locked crypto-assets on the protocol within hours.[79] Part 3.3.5, Leverage discusses the limited tools for resolving large positions in an orderly manner that may be available to DeFi protocols in particular due to reliance on automated liquidation and reservations or practical difficulties in resolving positions off-chain.

---

77 Testimony of Sam Bankman-Fried, Hearing Before the U.S. House Committee on Agriculture, May 12, 2022, at https://docs.house.gov/meetings/AG/AG00/20220512/114729/HHRG-117-AG00-Wstate-Bankman-FriedS-20220512.pdf.

78 Igor Makarov and Antoinette Schoar. "Blockchain Analysis of the Bitcoin Market" NBER Working Paper 29396, at https://www.nber.org/papers/w29396.

79 Macauley Peterson, "$.2 Billion Withdrawn from AAVE's Money Market Protocol," *Blockworks*, October 29, 2021, at https://blockworks.co/4-2-billion-withdrawn-from-aaves-money-market-protocol/.

Box B: Three Arrows Capital

This box describes public reports regarding financial distress at the hedge fund Three Arrows Capital (3AC). 3AC filed for Chapter 15 bankruptcy protection in the United States on July 1, 2022, days after its liquidation was ordered by a court in the British Virgin Islands. Its distress reportedly had substantial ripple effects across crypto-asset markets beginning in June 2022.[80] Market commentators viewed the episode as illustrating the vulnerabilities presented by extensive interconnections among crypto-asset market participants.[81]

Several counterparties of 3AC reportedly suffered sizable losses. Voyager Digital, a publicly listed crypto-assets platform, had reportedly made a sizable loan to 3AC, constituting about 60 percent of Voyager Digital's total loan book as of year-end 2021.[82] Following reports of 3AC's financial distress, Voyager Digital imposed limits on withdrawals by its customers, raised funds through a credit line, and later filed for bankruptcy protections and announced a restructuring plan.[83] Other lenders that suffered losses on loans to 3AC reportedly included Blockchain.com, BlockFi, Deribit, and Genesis.[84] Market participants viewed 3AC's failure as likely contributing to downward price pressures on stETH, a crypto-asset offered by the Lido Finance platform representing Ether staked in Lido in preparation for changes to the Ethereum network. 3AC appeared to have engaged in large sales of stETH in order to raise funds at a time when the market for stETH was already somewhat illiquid.[85] **Figure B-1** displays these and some of the other entities that reportedly had exposures to 3AC.

80 MacKenzie Siaglos, "From $10 billion to zero: How a crypto hedge fund collapsed and dragged many investors down with it" *CNBC*, July 11, 2022, at https://www.cnbc.com/2022/07/11/how-the-fall-of-three-arrows-or-3ac-dragged-down-crypto-investors.html.

81 Emily Nicolle and Olga Kharif, "A $2 Trillion Free-Fall Rattles Crypto to the Core" *Bloomberg*, June 26, 2022, at https://www.bloomberg.com/news/articles/2022-06-26/crypto-winter-why-this-bitcoin-bear-market-is-different-from-the-past.

82 "Voyager Digital Commences Financial Restructuring Process to Maximize Value for All Stakeholders," press release, July 6, 2022, at https://www.investvoyager.com/pressreleases/voyager-digital-commences-financial-restructuring-process-to-maximize-value-for-all-stakeholders.

83 Eliot Brown and Yifan Wang, "Crypto Broker Voyager Digital Files for Bankruptcy Protection," *The Wall Street Journal*, July 6, 2022, at https://www.wsj.com/articles/crypto-broker-voyager-digital-files-for-bankruptcy-protection-11657098630.

84 Yueqi Yang, Lucca De Paoli, and Benjamin Roberson, "Blockchain.com Cooperating With Investigations Into Three Arrows" *Bloomberg*, June 30, 2022, at https://www.bloomberg.com/news/articles/2022-06-30/blockchain-com-cooperating-with-investigations-into-three-arrows?sref=PHkj6DsL. Danny Nelson, "BlockFi Liquidated Three Arrows Capital: Report" *CoinDesk*, June 16, 2022, at https://www.coindesk.com/business/2022/06/16/blockfi-liquidated-three-arrows-capital-report/. Scott Chipolina, "Deribit claims crypto hedge fund Three Arrows failed to repay $80mn" *Financial Times*, July 1, 2022, at https://www.ft.com/content/09f2cb5a-5e2d-4b5f-96cd-ffed455ae23b. Yueqi Yang, "Crypto Lender Genesis Confirms Exposure to Bankrupt Three Arrows Capital," *Bloomberg*, July 6, 2022, at https://www.bloomberg.com/news/articles/2022-07-06/crypto-lender-genesis-confirms-exposure-to-three-arrows-capital.

85 Anthonia Isichei, "Three Arrows Capital Sells Over 56,000 Staked Ether Amid Growing stETH Discount" crypto.news, June 14, 2022, at https://crypto.news/three-arrows-capital-56000-staked-ether-steth-discount/.

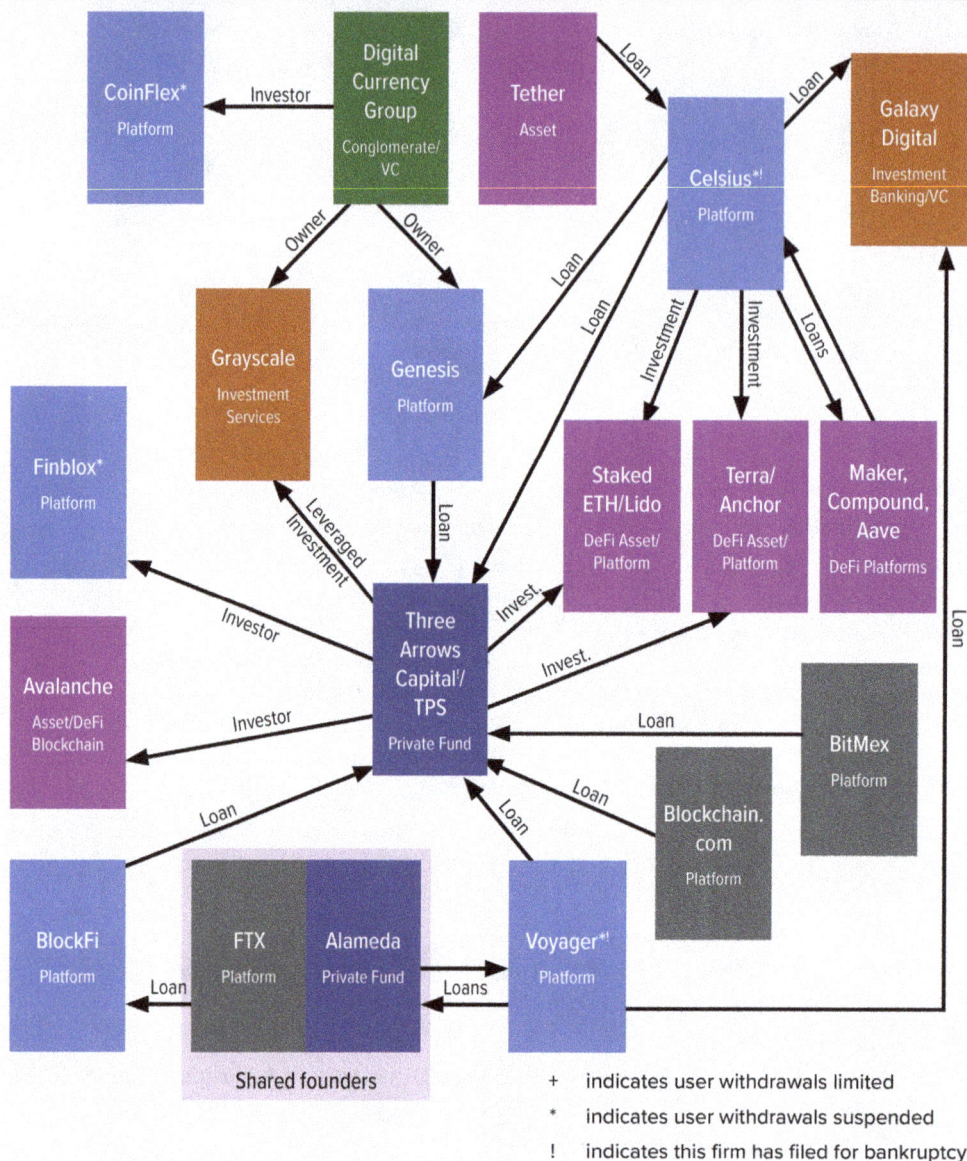

Figure B-1: Reported Interconnections of Three Arrows Capital

+   indicates user withdrawals limited
*   indicates user withdrawals suspended
!   indicates this firm has filed for bankruptcy

Notes: The information in this figure is from public reports and is not comprehensive. Additional interconnections between firms and other market participants are likely.

3AC reportedly had a wide range of investments, as also illustrated by **Figure B-1**.[86] This figure details public reports about loans or investments made by 3AC, loans made to 3AC, and similar interconnections among those that have direct connections to 3AC. Commentators have suggested that a key contributor to 3AC's financial distress

---

86   Verified Petition under Chapter 15 for Recognition of a Foreign Main Proceeding and Related Relief, In re: Three Arrows Capital, Ltd., No. 22-10920-mg (Bnkr. S.D.N.Y. July 1, 2022).

came from the collapsed value of its holdings of Luna, a crypto-asset affiliated with TerraUSD stablecoin and a central component of its purported stabilization mechanism.[87] Commentators have also pointed to losses from a leveraged arbitrage bet related to the price of Bitcoin in comparison to the price of Grayscale Bitcoin Trust, which only holds Bitcoin.[88] 3AC has stated that it had investments in several other crypto-asset projects, including DeFi protocols, blockchains, video games and NFTs, and investments in other investment funds.[89] In addition, Finblox, a staking DeFi protocol that had received investments from 3AC, imposed withdrawal limits as it evaluated the impact of 3AC's distress on liquidity and market conditions.[90]

3.3.3 Operational Vulnerabilities

Operational vulnerabilities involve key market activities or infrastructure that are likely to be disrupted in a response to a shock, such as a malicious attack or some other unexpected development. Operational vulnerabilities generally pertain to the disruptions in the ability of market participants to conduct their normal financial activities, in contrast to interconnections that generally pertain to losses market participants would bear from financial exposure to a key counterparty.

In the crypto-asset ecosystem, several different types of operational activities or infrastructures appear to underpin the functioning of the crypto-assets market.[91] In addition, the basic infrastructure of crypto-assets, such as distributed ledger technologies, may be vulnerable to disruption. Malicious attacks could be one

87 Shaurya Malwa, "Three Arrows Capital Confirms Heavy Losses From LUNA's Collapse, Exploring Potential Options: Report," *CoinDesk*, June 17, 2022, at https://www.coindesk.com/business/2022/06/17/three-arrows-capital-confirms-heavy-losses-from-lunas-collapse-exploring-potential-options-report/. Declaration of Russell Crumpler in Support of Verified Petition under Chapter 15 for Recognition of a Foreign Main Proceeding and Related Relief, In re: Three Arrows Capital, Ltd., No. 22-10920-mg (Bankr. S.D.N.Y. July 1, 2022).

88 Joanna Ossinger, Muyao Shen, and Yueqi Yang, "Three Arrows Founders Break Silence Over Collapse of Crypto Hedge Fund," *Bloomberg*, July 22, 2022, at https://www.bloomberg.com/news/articles/2022-07-22/three-arrows-founders-en-route-to-dubai-describe-ltcm-moment?sref=PHkj6DsL.

89 *See* Three Arrows Capital, "Select Investments," Accessed July 31, 2022, at https://www.threearrowscap.com/select-investments/.

90 Oliver Knight, "Finblox Raises Withdrawal Limit, Explores Legal Action Against Three Arrow Capital," *CoinDesk*, July 1, 2022, at https://www.coindesk.com/business/2022/07/01/finblox-raises-withdrawal-limit-explores-legal-action-against-three-arrows-capital/.

91 *See, e.g.,* Evan Sultanik et al., Trail of Bits, *Are Blockchains Decentralized? Unintended Centralities in Distributed Ledgers*, June 2022, at https://assets-global.website-files.com/5fd11235b3950c2c1a3b6df4/62af6c641a672b3329b9a480_Unintended_Centralities_in_Distributed_Ledgers.pdf. Evan Sultanik and Mike Meyers, Trail of Bits, *Do You Really Need a Blockchain? An Operational Risk Assessment*, June 2022, at https://uploads-ssl.webflow.com/5fd11235b3950c2c1a3b6df4/62b53d560764fa44279445ff_Blockchain_Operational_Risk_Assessment.pdf.

source of such disruption; that subject is discussed in more detail in part 3.6, Sources of Shocks.

Distributed Ledger Technology

Distributed ledger technology on which crypto-asset activities are built may be subject to operational vulnerabilities. In a permissionless system, when market participants interact with blockchains they may be exposed to potential disruptions caused by bugs in the underlying code and that may be difficult to patch in a timely manner, or at all, due to the permissionless nature of the ledger. In permissioned systems, participants may be exposed to disruptions created by coding changes implemented by the central entity that controls the system.[92]

Mining, Validation, and Blockchain Maintenance

The mining, validation, and maintenance of blockchains tends to be highly concentrated. As a result, even though many activities in crypto-asset markets are distributed, there is concentration in practice among key participants such as miners, validators, and other maintenance roles. This concentration may present a vulnerability since it causes the activities to be more easily susceptible to disruption from a technological outage, operational error, or malicious attack. Altogether, concentration of mining, validation, and blockchain maintenance may create similar risks to concentration of third-party service providers in traditional finance, though the risks may be intensified by the lack of formal relationships between entities that depend on these activities and the participants who engage in them. Indeed, though many crypto-asset activities are described as non-intermediated, miners and validators may be viewed as intermediaries in the ability of market participants to engage in crypto-asset activities.[93]

Concentration of mining and validation appears to be a result of the fixed costs of both PoW and PoS arrangements, creating increasing returns to scale.[94] In PoW protocols, pooling of mining resources also increases available computing power, increasing the probability of successful mining. Pooling can also provide co-insurance across members of a pool in either PoS or PoW, regarding the probability of being chosen to complete a certain transaction and earn associated rewards. Research has found very high degrees of concentration in Bitcoin mining in the

---

92 Evan Sultanik et al., Trail of Bits, *Are Blockchains Decentralized? Unintended Centralities in Distributed Ledgers*, June 2022, at https://assets-global.website-files.com/5fd11235b3950c2c1a3b6 df4/62af6c641a672b3329b9a480_Unintended_Centralities_in_Distributed_Ledgers.pdf.

93 Raphael Auer, Jon Frost and Jose Maria Vidal Pastor, "Miners as intermediaries: extractable value and market manipulation in crypto and DeFi", BIS, June 16, 2022, at https://www.bis.org/publ/ bisbull58.pdf.

94 Igor Makarov and Antoinette Schoar, "Cryptocurrencies and Decentralized Finance," NBER Working Paper 30006, 2022, at https://www.nber.org/papers/w30006.

first few years after its launch.[95] Additional research found that in the five years leading up to 2021, Bitcoin mining capacity continued to be highly concentrated, with the top 10 percent of miners controlling 90 percent of mining capacity and just 0.1 percent of miners (about 50 miners) controlling close to 50 percent of mining capacity.[96] Likewise, the number of maintainers for the Bitcoin blockchain has been very low.[97] Similarly, high levels of concentration have been found for other blockchains that employ PoW, including Ethereum, Litecoin, Bitcoin Cash, and DASH.[98] The concentration of PoS validators has also been very high. Among the largest proof-of-stake protocols, the top 10 validators reportedly have typically held more than 25 percent of capacity, while the top 50 validators have held more than 50 percent. [99]

A related risk associated with mining and validation is the potential for collusion. Researchers have found, in theory, that generating decentralized consensus leads to incentives for collusive activity.[100]

Miners and validators must be given appropriate incentives to process a transaction in order for the network to be appropriately maintained. These incentives come in the form of rewards or fees, which can vary depending on network congestion. For example, on the Ethereum network, the payments made by market participants in order to complete a transaction are known as gas fees. A transaction may not be processed if the originator does not offer to pay a high enough gas fee. During times of market stress, congestion may be high, reducing the ability of participants to complete transactions or raising the cost of transactions significantly, creating potentially significant operational issues. **Figure 10** shows that Ethereum gas fees

---

95 Alyssa Blackburn et al., "Cooperation among an anonymous group protected Bitcoin during failures of decentralization," Working paper, at https://aidenlab.org/bitcoin.pdf.

96 Igor Makarov and Antoinette Schoar. "Blockchain Analysis of the Bitcoin Market" NBER Working Paper 29396, at https://www.nber.org/papers/w29396.

97 Evan Sultanik et al., Trail of Bits, Are Blockchains Decentralized? Unintended Centralities in Distributed Ledgers, June 2022, at https://assets-global.website-files.com/5fd11235b3950c2c1a3 b6df4/62af6c641a672b3329b9a480_Unintended_Centralities_in_Distributed_Ledgers.pdf. Evan Sultanik and Mike Meyers, Trail of Bits, *Do You Really Need a Blockchain? An Operational Risk Assessment*, June 2022, at https://uploads-ssl.webflow.com/5fd11235b3950c2c1a3b6df4/62b53d56 0764fa44279445ff_Blockchain_Operational_Risk_Assessment.pdf.

98   Igor Makarov and Antoinette Schoar, "Cryptocurrencies and Decentralized Finance," NBER Working Paper 30006, 2022. at https://www.nber.org/papers/w30006.

99 Igor Makarov and Antoinette Schoar, "Cryptocurrencies and Decentralized Finance," NBER Working Paper 30006, 2022, at https://www.nber.org/papers/w30006. The proof-of-stake blockchains analyzed are Solana, Cardano, Avalanche, Terra, Polkadot, Cosmos Hub, NEAR Protocol, Polygon, Fantom, and Tezos. The data exclude Ethereum, which at the time of this working paper's publication was preparing for transition to proof-of-stake.

100 Cong, Lin William, and Zhiguo He. "Blockchain disruption and smart contracts." *The Review of Financial Studies* vol. 32 no. 5, 2019, pp. 1754-1797, at https://academic.oup.com/rfs/article-abstra ct/32/5/1754/5427778?redirectedFrom=fulltext.

have occasionally risen to very high levels. As an example of the disruption that could result from high transaction costs, if a market participant with a leveraged position desired to post additional collateral to meet a margin call, they may not be able to complete that transaction, and instead their position may be liquidated. High fees may be "a feature, not a bug" if validators use their market power to extract economic rents from crypto-asset markets.[101]

Figure 10: Average Daily Transaction, or "Gas," Fees on the Ethereum Network

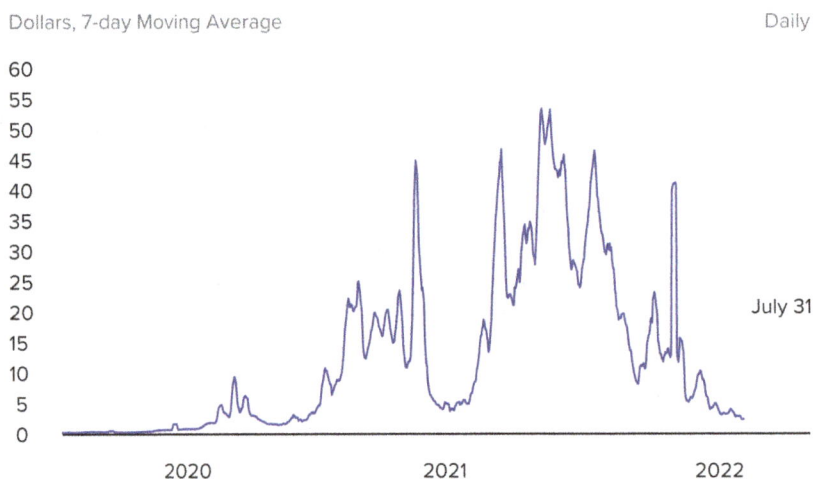

Source: Etherscan.io

Mining operations appear to depend on the spread miners can earn between the price of the assets they mine and the variable cost of mining, such as electricity costs. As a result, miners appear vulnerable to procyclical financial pressure. Miners earn rewards in a blockchain's native crypto-asset, such as Bitcoin in the case of the Bitcoin blockchain. When the price of the crypto-asset falls, miners may take mining capacity offline unless there is a corresponding reduction in mining costs, which are denominated in national currency rather than crypto-asset. As an example of miners coming under financial pressures, some commercial miners disclosed that they sold more Bitcoin than they mined amidst falling prices in the spring of 2022, in part to address their debt loads.[102] In addition, these financial pressures may cause concentration and congestion to increase when prices fall. Potentially, if substantial mining capacity were to go offline due to lower crypto-asset prices, transaction

---

101 Hyun Song Shin, "The future monetary system" June 26, 2022, at https://www.bis.org/speeches/sp220626b_slides.pdf.

102 Stacy Elliott, "Public Bitcoin Miners Are Selling Off BTC Reserves as Crypto Winter Sets In," *Decrypt*, June 22, 2022. https://decrypt.co/103539/public-bitcoin-miners-selling-btc-reserves-crypto-winter.

throughput could decline and validation times could rise, reducing the attractiveness of related crypto-asset activities and further reducing asset prices. As a result, mining may be vulnerable not just to conventional technological outages but also to disruption due to the economic incentives of miners, including electricity costs and debt loads. Since these disruptions could occur simultaneously with increases in trading volume as investors try to exit crypto-asset positions due to falling prices, miners may not be available to process transactions and market participants may not be able to conduct transactions.

Additional risks related to mining and validation include reliance on miners and validators who may not be in compliance with relevant laws. Market participants cannot choose which miner validates a transaction and, therefore, cannot choose to avoid a miner if the miner is anonymous or a sanctioned entity. Some industry participants have opposed sanctions compliance at the base infrastructure level by issuing policy papers or funding lawsuits challenging sanctions determinations,[103] while others have focused on the operational implications that may be created by a lack of sanctions and illicit finance checks by miners and validators.[104]

Providers of Infrastructure

A small number of infrastructure providers serve broad swaths of the crypto-asset ecosystem. Large parts of the crypto-asset ecosystem—including developers, platforms, and individual participants—rely on infrastructure providers for key services in what is sometimes referred to as a "blockchain-as-a-service" model. For example, firms may provide security, front-end access to decentralized applications, support blockchain operations, or develop non-custodial wallets. These service providers offer developer tools and application programming interfaces (APIs) that can be integrated into other firms' operations. Because distributed ledger activities tend to be modular, building on top of other existing activities, many activities ultimately rely on a small number of key infrastructure providers. [105] In practice, market observers have noted that market participants tend to rely on infrastructure providers.[106] This reliance entails significant operational risks if the providers do

---

103 *See, e.g.* Rodrigo Seira, Amy Aixi Zhang, Dan Robinson, "Base Layer Neutrality," Paradigm, September 8, 2022, at https://www.paradigm.xyz/2022/09/base-layer-neutrality and Brian Armstrong, "Defending Privacy in Crypto", September 8, 2022 at https://blog.coinbase.com/defending-privacy-in-crypto-e09db33dece8.

104 Nicholas Weaver, "OFAC Around and Find Out," Lawfare, August 19, 2022, at https://www.lawfareblog.com/ofac-around-and-find-out.

105 *See, e.g.* Scott Nover, "The Decentralized Web Is Not Decentralized," Quartz, January 19, 2022, at https://qz.com/2112965/web3-is-not-decentralized/.

106 "My first impressions of web3", January 7, 2022, at https://moxie.org/2022/01/07/web3-first-impressions.html.

not conform to current standards for cybersecurity and operational resilience.[107] As a result of service providers centralizing many pieces of infrastructure in practice, that infrastructure is vulnerable to disruption if a key service provider experiences a disruption from a system outage or a malicious attack. As an example, a delayed software update at a leading node operator on the Ethereum network in November 2020 caused prolonged and widespread disruption on numerous crypto-asset platforms.[108]

Key Operational Services Provided by Platforms

Platforms offer a number of key operational services to crypto-asset market participants. Platforms have experienced disruptions from time to time, and those disruptions have the potential to have knock-on implications for market participants that rely on those services. These services include the custody and safekeeping of private keys, trade facilitation, maintaining order books, market making, and margin lending. In addition to operational risks, the interconnection risks of platforms are discussed in part 3.3.2, Financial Exposures via Interconnections within the Crypto-Asset Ecosystem.

Stablecoins

Stablecoins provide a key operational service supporting speculative trading, lending and borrowing among platforms, and protocols. Participants in crypto-asset markets may perceive stablecoins as liquid, price stable, and providing fast execution, and therefore use them as a leg in many transactions. Disruptions to stablecoin arrangements therefore would likely have substantial effects on the ability of market participants to trade, lend, and borrow. The IOSCO Decentralized Finance Report identified certain sources of potential disruptions to stablecoin services.[109] In addition to operational risks, the run risks of stablecoins are discussed in part 3.3.4, Funding Mismatches and Risk of Runs, and the risks related to potential interconnections with the traditional financial system are discussed in part 3.2, Interconnections with the Traditional Financial System.

---

107 For a discussion of such standards, see Exec. Order No. 14028, 86 Fed. Reg. 26633 (May 17, 2022), at https://www.govinfo.gov/content/pkg/FR-2021-05-17/pdf/2021-10460.pdf.

108 Infura, "Infura Mainnet Outage Post-Morterm," November 11, 2020, at https://blog.infura.io/post/infura-mainnet-outage-post-mortem-2020-11-11.

109 IOSCO, "IOSCO Decentralized Finance Report," March 2022, at https://www.iosco.org/library/pubdocs/pdf/IOSCOPD699.pdf.

Wallets and Custody Services

Wallets provide a variety of services to users that are key to the functioning of crypto-asset markets, including facilitating the transfer of crypto-assets between users.[110] Wallets may be self-hosted; alternatively, wallets may be custodial, in which users rely on a custodial wallet provider to hold crypto-assets on their behalf. Provision of these services may be concentrated, creating operational vulnerabilities if a major wallet provider were to experience a disruption, such as a hack. In such a situation, customers may not be able to access their crypto-assets and otherwise function normally.

3.3.4 Funding Mismatches and Risk of Runs

Runs can occur in response to a shock if investors reassess the safety of their funds and abruptly seek to withdraw their investments. Financial institutions may need to sell assets quickly at "fire sale" prices, particularly if they promise speedy returns of funds at par while engaging in maturity or liquidity transformation, absent sufficient liquidity backstops and appropriate regulation. Fire sales can cause those institutions to bear substantial losses and potentially put downward pressure on key asset markets. Runs can also occur due to fears of insolvency even without a fire sale. Though sentiment often plays a key role in bringing about runs, investors can have a rational motivation to withdraw if they perceive the ability to avoid losses that are borne by other investors.

Runs are an endemic feature of financial history. A variety of financial institutions over time have engaged in liquidity or maturity transformation while promising or allowing withdrawals upon demand. Many such cases have ended in severe economic harm for millions of Americans, financial disruption, and policy reforms. American financial regulators and policymakers have spent generations working to reduce the frequency of runs including by implementing capital and financial reporting, engaging in prudent governance, risk management, and audit and internal control practices, subjecting firms to liquidity regulations, conducting prudential supervision to increase the resiliency of financial institutions and confidence in them, introducing deposit insurance, and developing lender of last resort facilities. These features are broadly absent from the crypto-asset ecosystem, and consequently runs, withdrawal restrictions, failures, and panics have occurred in crypto-asset markets at a high frequency.

Stablecoins have acute vulnerabilities to runs if not paired with appropriate governance, risk management, financial reporting, auditing and internal control standards, capital and liquidity standards, and regulation. Run risk may exist in varying degrees depending on the stabilization method or the assets purportedly held by the stablecoin. The scale and potential impact of run risks associated with

---

110 For further discussion of wallets, see Congressional Research Service, "Digital Wallets and Selected Policy Issues" April 18, 2022, at https://crsreports.congress.gov/product/pdf/IF/IF12079.

stablecoins have increased with the substantial growth of the reported market capitalization of stablecoins over the past couple of years, as shown in **Figure 11**.

Figure 11: Reported Market Capitalization of Major Stablecoins

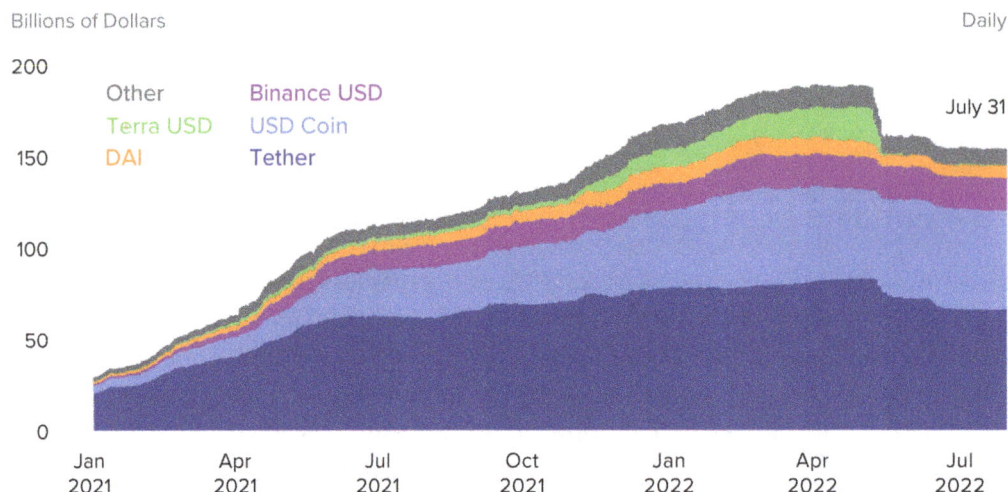

Source: DeFi Llama

The run on, and collapse of, the TerraUSD stablecoin in May 2022 as shown in **Figure 11**, is discussed in Box C. The episode also appears to have led to a temporary and less catastrophic run on the Tether stablecoin and appears to have had broader impacts on crypto market activities. A year earlier, the Iron stablecoin also suffered a run and completely collapsed. More recently, the HUSD stablecoin also temporarily lost its peg.[111] In their relatively brief history, algorithmic stablecoins already appear to be vulnerable to runs, and other stablecoins have also shown run risks.

In addition, platforms are vulnerable to runs on funds they receive from investors. In mid-2022, market commentators described a wave of runs that led to a number of platforms restricting customers' ability to withdraw invested funds, including Babel Finance, Celsius, Coinloan, Coinflex, Finblox, Hodlnaut, Vauld, Voyager Digital, and Zipmex.[112] Celsius and Voyager Digital filed for bankruptcy protections, which press

---

111 Oliver Knight, "Cash-backed HUSD Stablecoin loses Peg, Drops to 92 Cents" *CoinDesk*, August 18, 2022, at https://www.coindesk.com/markets/2022/08/18/cash-backed-husd-stablecoin-loses-peg-drops-to-092/.

112 Jimmy He, "Want to Strike Terror in Crypto Markets in 2022? Just Say You're Suspending Withdrawals" *CoinDesk*, August 3, 2022, at https://www.coindesk.com/markets/2022/08/03/want-to-strike-terror-in-crypto-markets-in-2022-just-say-youre-suspending-withdrawals/. Yiwen Lu, "Hodlnaut becomes the latest crypto lender to block withdrawals" *The Washington Post*, August 9, 2022, at https://www.washingtonpost.com/business/2022/08/09/hodlnaut-suspends-withdrawals/.

reports described as further affecting millions of their customers' abilities to retrieve invested funds.[113]

Custody providers may also be vulnerable to run pressures. Many platforms represent that they are providing custody services and holding private keys or traditional financial assets in a manner such that the assets remain the property of the customer. In theory, these arrangements would mitigate run risk by assuring customers of the full return of their custodied assets. In the event of a platform's bankruptcy, it is possible that customer assets would not be part of the bankruptcy estate. If so, customers would be able to access and withdraw their assets, though some delay may still apply. Whether this would occur in practice, however, depends on the precise nature of the purported custodial relationship and the bankruptcy court's view of the crypto-assets. Some courts could view customers as unsecured creditors in bankruptcy. As noted in part 3.3.2, Financial Exposures via Interconnections within The Crypto-Asset Ecosystem, at least one major crypto-asset platform has acknowledged that customer funds, which are commingled with the funds of the platform, may be considered the property of the bankruptcy estate in the event of insolvency.

Box C: The Collapse of the TerraUSD Stablecoin

This box details public reports regarding the collapse of the TerraUSD stablecoin in May 2022, which illustrates financial stability risks associated with runs and interconnections.

Background

Entering into May 2022, TerraUSD was the third largest stablecoin globally, with a market capitalization estimated to be over $18 billion.[114] TerraUSD purportedly was designed as an algorithmic stablecoin, that would maintain a stable value without the use of non-crypto-asset reserve assets. TerraUSD's value rested on its convertibility into one dollar worth of Luna, an affiliated "governance token" on the Terra blockchain. The mechanism was purported to give market participants the incentive to drive the value of Terra to one dollar, either by exchanging TerraUSD for Luna if the former was worth less than a dollar, or vice versa.[115] In addition, though promoters of TerraUSD described it as "decentralized," a group known as the Luna Foundation Guard—organized in 2022 by the CEO of Terraform Labs, which had developed TerraUSD—had also reportedly acquired $3.5 billion worth of Bitcoin

---

113 Becky Yerak and Akiko Matsuda, "For Crypto Customers, a Long Battle Ahead in Bankruptcy," *The Wall Street Journal*, August 1, 2022, at https://www.wsj.com/articles/for-crypto-customers-a-long-battle-ahead-in-bankruptcy-11659379620.

114 https://coinmarketcap.com/currencies/terrausd/historical-data/

115 Muyao Shen, "How $60 Billion in Terra Coins Went Up in Algorithmic Smoke," *Bloomberg*, May 20, 2022, at https://www.bloomberg.com/graphics/2022-crypto-luna-terra-stablecoin-explainer/.

by May 2022 to be used to stabilize the value of Terra if needed.[116] Reports do not suggest that typical holders of TerraUSD had the ability to directly redeem TerraUSD for Bitcoin.

TerraUSD's reported market capitalization grew rapidly from late 2021 through May 2022, in tandem with Luna's price and the volume of activity on various DeFi protocols on the Terra Blockchain. Luna was as high as the seventh largest crypto-asset as of early April 2022, with a reported market capitalization of $41 billion.[117] TerraUSD reportedly was used to support the operations of more than one hundred DeFi platforms on the Terra blockchain offering services like borrowing and lending of crypto-assets, insurance, and synthetic securities.[118] That said, the largest use for the Terra blockchain was reportedly the Anchor protocol, launched by Terraform Labs, which purported to pay out high interest rates on investments of TerraUSD.[119] One DeFi data source states Anchor reached more than $17 billion of total value locked by early May 2022.[120]

The Collapse of TerraUSD

Public reports cite several factors that may have contributed to the collapse of TerraUSD, including nervousness about its stabilization mechanism, doubts about the Anchor protocol, and temporarily limited liquidity, but generally express uncertainty about the major proximate causes or underlying forces behind them.[121] Regardless, on May 9th, the market price of TerraUSD declined substantially below its purported dollar peg, as shown in **Figure C-1**. Several platforms halted trading of TerraUSD, and in the following days, the price of TerraUSD declined further to nearly zero. **Figure C-2** shows the decline in the market capitalization of TerraUSD and Luna.

---

116 Tom Robinson, "What Happened to the $3.5 Billion Terra Reserve? Elliptic Follows the Bitcoin," *Elliptic*, May 13, 2022, at https://www.elliptic.co/blog/what-happened-to-the-3.5-billion-terra-reserve-elliptic-follows-the-bitcoins.

117 https://web.archive.org/web/20220404035202/https://coinmarketcap.com/

118 Krisztian Sandor, "What is LUNA and UST? A Guide to the Terra Ecosystem" *CoinDesk*, May 9, 2022, at https://www.coindesk.com/learn/what-is-luna-and-ust-a-guide-to-the-terra-ecosystem/.

119 Liam J. Kelly, "We Need to Talk About Terra's Anchor" *Decrypt*, April 23, 2022, at https://decrypt.co/98482/we-need-to-talk-about-terras-anchor.

120 https://defillama.com/protocol/anchor

121   Muyao Shen, "How $60 Billion in Terra Coins Went Up in Algorithmic Smoke," *Bloomberg*, May 20, 2022, at https://www.bloomberg.com/graphics/2022-crypto-luna-terra-stablecoin-explainer.

Figure C-1: Prices of Luna and TerraUSD

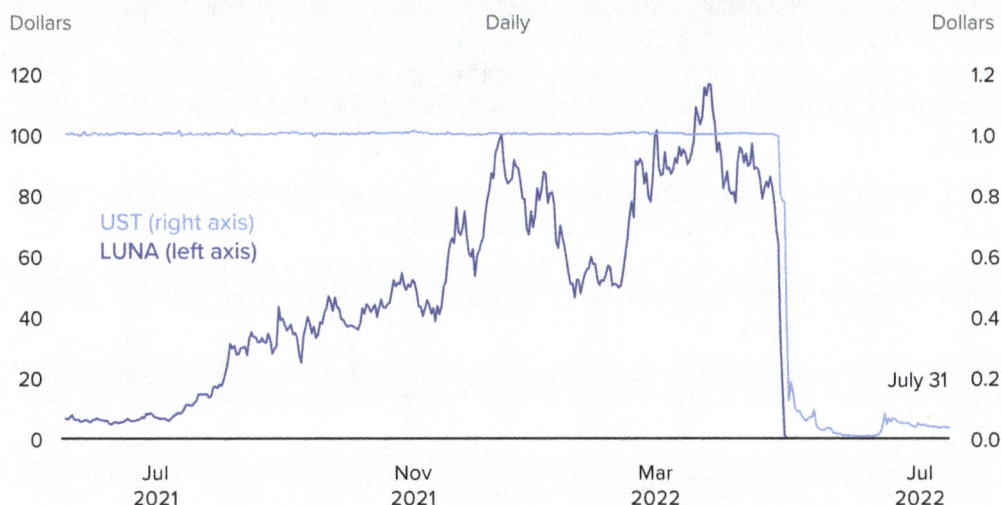

Source: Coingecko

Figure C-2: Market Capitalization of Luna and TerraUSD

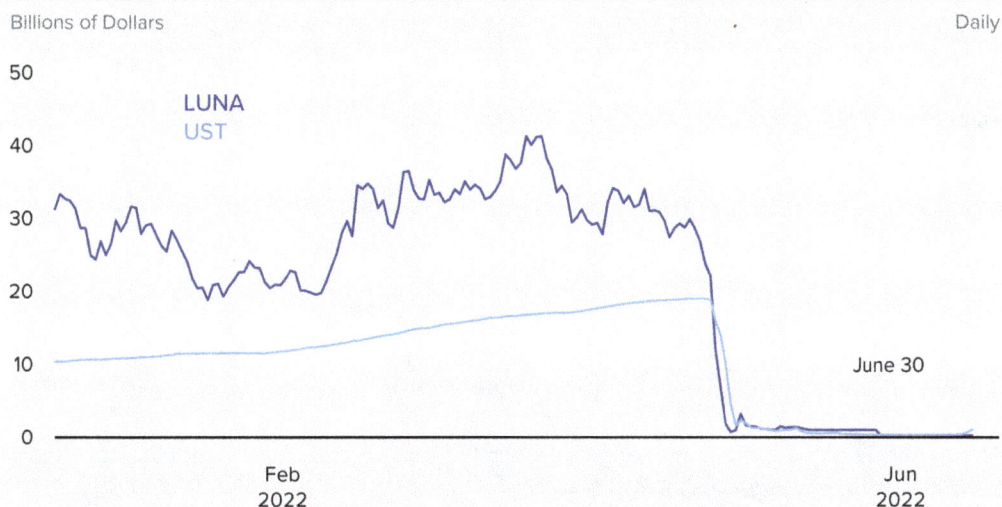

Source: Coingecko

Commentary has emphasized that the credibility of TerraUSD's stabilization mechanism rested on its affiliated crypto-asset, Luna, having a non-zero value, and that Luna appears to have had an excessively high price driven by speculation. [122]

---

122 Matt Levine, "Terra Flops," *Bloomberg*, May 11, 2022, at https://www.bloomberg.com/opinion/articles/2022-05-11/terra-flops.

Illustration of Financial Stability Risks

The U.S. economy's traditional financial markets have continued to function following turmoil in crypto-assets during 2022, as overall crypto-assets remain sufficiently small in scale and unconnected with the traditional financial system to pose significant financial stability risks. However, the rapid collapse of TerraUSD and subsequent events may illustrate important vulnerabilities inside the crypto-asset ecosystem.

Market commentators have suggested that TerraUSD's collapse triggered a depegging of, and subsequent run on, Tether, the largest stablecoin globally.[123] In contrast to TerraUSD's algorithmic stabilization mechanism, Tether's dollar peg is purportedly "backed" by off-chain holdings of traditional financial system assets.[124] On May 11, Tether's price on the secondary market reached a low of $0.94, or about $0.97-$0.98 as measured on an hourly frequency as shown in **Figure C-3**, before recovering to slightly below $1.00 within a day. Tether's market capitalization declined from roughly $83 billion before the event to about $74 billion on May 18.

Figure C-3: Prices of Tether and USDC

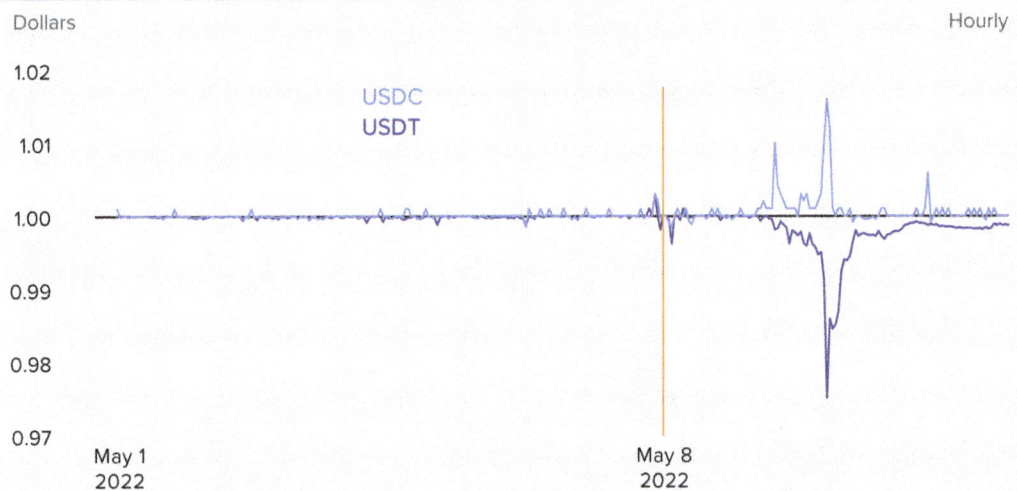

Source: Cryptocompare

The run on Tether coincided with an increase in the price and supply of another stablecoin, USDC, as shown in **Figures C-3** and **C-4**.

---

123 Brian Laverdure, "How the TerraUSD Collapse is Affecting Financial Markets," Independent Community Bankers of America, June 7, 2022, at https://www.icba.org/newsroom/blogs/main-street-matters/2022/06/07/how-the-terrausd-collapse-is-affecting-financial-markets.

124 https://tether.to/en/transparency/#reports

Figure C-4: Outstanding Supply of Tether and USDC

Billions of Tokens   Daily   Billions of Tokens

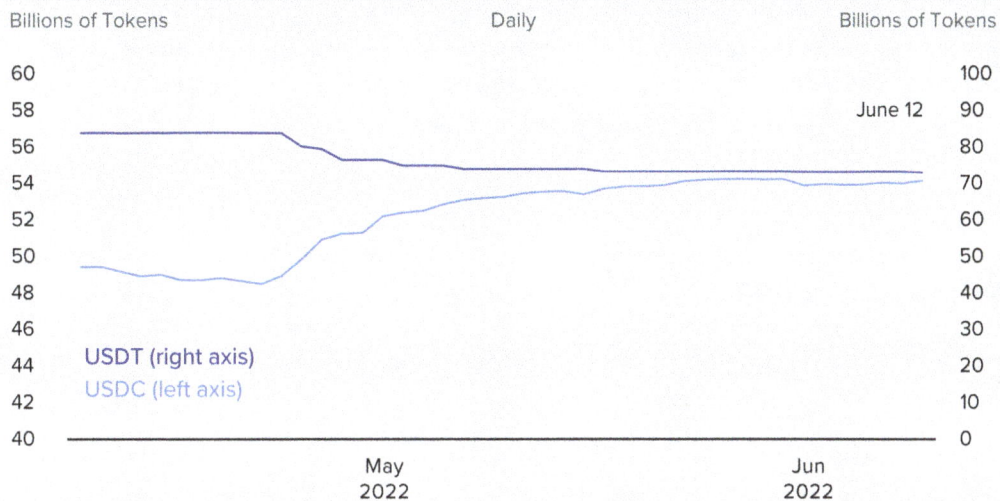

June 12

USDT (right axis)
USDC (left axis)

May
2022

Jun
2022

Source: CryptoCompare

The runs on TerraUSD and Tether illustrates that risk of runs can arise in different ways. Algorithmic stablecoins are subject to run risks if owners of those crypto-assets perceive a weakness in the stabilization mechanism and seek to sell their holding before its price collapses further. Investors may also have the incentive to run if they doubt a stablecoin issuer has sufficient assets to meet all its liabilities or could lack assets after a fire sale. In the case of Tether, financial regulators and others have criticized the veracity of Tether's asset attestations.[125] Market commentators have suggested that Tether's opacity about its asset holdings and the potential duration and liquidity mismatch of its assets with its liabilities likely contributed to the run it experienced in May 2022.[126]

TerraUSD's collapse may also illustrate vulnerabilities presented by interconnections, though such interconnections are difficult to observe or measure, given opacity in crypto-asset markets. Some interconnected market participants reportedly lost substantial sums on their investments in TerraUSD, Luna, or affiliated projects, including Three Arrows

125 New York Attorney General, "Attorney General James Ends Virtual Currency Trading Platform Bitfinex's Illegal Activities in New York," February 23, 2021, at https://ag.ny.gov/press-release/2021/attorney-general-james-ends-virtual-currency-trading-platform-bitfinexs-illegal. CFTC, "CFTC Orders Tether and Bitfinex to Pay Fines Totaling $42.5 Million," October 15, 2021, at https://www.cftc.gov/PressRoom/PressReleases/8450-21.

126 David Yaffe-Bellany, "The Coin That Could Wreck Crypto," *The New York Times*, June 17, 2022, at https://www.nytimes.com/2022/06/17/technology/tether-stablecoin-cryptocurrency.html.

Capital (see Box B).[127] TerraUSD's collapse reportedly also impacted some other firms, including those involved in crypto-asset market making and in venture capital.[128]

In addition, the collapse of TerraUSD reportedly also had repercussions on other parts of the crypto-asset ecosystem. Total value locked in the DeFi protocol Anchor reportedly collapsed.[129] Commentators have suggested that the Luna Foundation Guard's liquidation of Bitcoin in an attempt to support TerraUSD, if it occurred, may have contributed to downward pressure on Bitcoin prices.[130] Investors with substantial funds invested in the Anchor protocol reportedly included Celsius Networks.[131] Terra's collapse also appears to have impacted DeFi activities more broadly. As shown in **Figure C-5**, total value locked in DeFi protocols decreased even in protocols not based on the Terra blockchain following the collapse of TerraUSD.

---

127 Shaurya Malwa, "Three Arrows Capital Confirms Heavy Losses From LUNA's Collapse, Exploring Potential Options: Report," *CoinDesk*, June 17, 2022, at https://www.coindesk.com/business/2022/06/17/three-arrows-capital-confirms-heavy-losses-from-lunas-collapse-exploring-potential-options-report/. Declaration of Russell Crumpler in Support of Verified Petition under Chapter 15 for Recognition of a Foreign Main Proceeding and Related Relief, In re: Three Arrows Capital, Ltd., No. 22-10920-mg (Bankr. S.D.N.Y. July 1, 2022).

128 Scott Chipolina and George Steer, "The Terra/Luna hall of shame" *Financial Times*, May 25, 2022, at https://www.ft.com/content/40c06a4f-3586-40be-b5ad-b836b5dcdc0d. Katherine Doherty and Yueqi Yang, "As the Crypto Winter Hits Its Peers, Chicago Trading Firm Jump Is Ready for More Bets," *Bloomberg*, June 17, 2022, at https://www.bloomberg.com/news/articles/2022-06-17/jump-trading-prowls-for-edge-with-crypto-winter-hammering-peers. Hooyeon Kim, "Early Investor In Defunct Luna Token Plans to Raise Another Fund" *Bloomberg*, August 2, 2022, at https://www.bloomberg.com/news/articles/2022-08-02/early-investor-in-defunct-luna-token-plans-to-raise-another-fund.

129 "The Collapse of Anchor," Greythorn Asset Management, June 8, 2022, at https://www.greythorn.com/the-collapse-of-anchor.

130 David Yaffe-Bellany and Erin Griffith, "How a Trash-Talking Crypto Founder Caused a $40 Billion Crash," *The New York Times*, May 18, 2022, at https://www.nytimes.com/2022/05/18/technology/terra-luna-cryptocurrency-do-kwon.htmlLink.

131 Ryan Weeks, "Celsius Pulled Half A Billion Dollars Out of Anchor Protocol amid Terra Chaos," *The Block*, May 13, 2022, at https://www.theblock.co/post/146752/celsius-pulled-half-a-billion-dollars-out-of-anchor-protocol-amid-terra-chaos.

Figure C-5: Reported Total Value Locked in DeFi

Billions of dollars

Daily

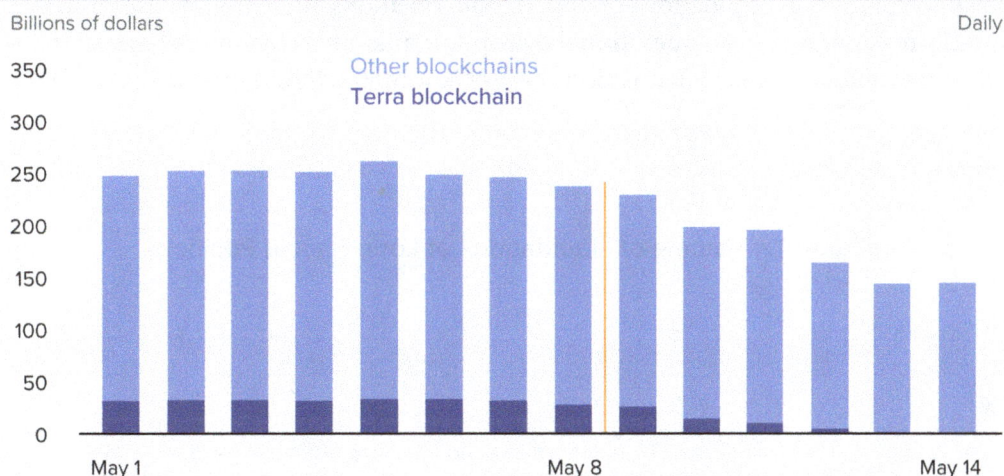

Source: DeFiLlama.

Notes: Total Value Locked is the overall value of assets committed to a DeFi protocol.

3.3.5 Leverage

The use of high amounts of leverage by financial market participants leaves them vulnerable to stress in response to a shock, such as poor news about a crypto-asset project or negative macroeconomic developments. Such a shock may cause the assets they own to fall in value or lead counterparties to demand that their leveraged positions be unwound. Abrupt or forced deleveraging can create waves of cascading liquidations that further propagate shocks. In addition, falling prices expose leveraged positions, and financial institutions and other counterparties may face elevated losses. In these ways, high leverage can amplify the volatility and procyclicality of asset price declines and market dynamics.

The exact nature of leverage present in crypto-asset markets is challenging to quantify, given opacity regarding the actual use of leverage. Nevertheless, very high and excessive amounts of leverage are likely present in the crypto-asset system, as judged by the impact that episodes of widespread deleveraging appear to have had on crypto-asset market conditions. Episodes of major crypto-asset price drops have tended to coincide with unusually large levels of liquidations on large crypto-asset trading platforms.[132] For example, a sharp drop in the price of Bitcoin in early 2020

---

132 *See* a discussion of advertised leverage and of liquidations by Sirio Aramonte, Wenqian Huang, and Andreas Schrimpf, "DeFi risks and the Decentralisation Illusion," BIS, December 2021, at https://www.bis.org/publ/qtrpdf/r_qt2112b.pdf.

reportedly occurred amidst an unusually high volume of liquidations.[133] **Figure 12** shows that drops in Bitcoin prices over late 2021 and 2022 coincided with very elevated volumes of liquidations of long Bitcoin positions. In extreme cases in which a platform experienced an operational disruption, platform customers have stated they were unable to close out positions before automated liquidation occurred.[134]

Leverage is available to crypto-assets market participants through several different venues.

Figure 12: Volume of Liquidations of Long Bitcoin Positions

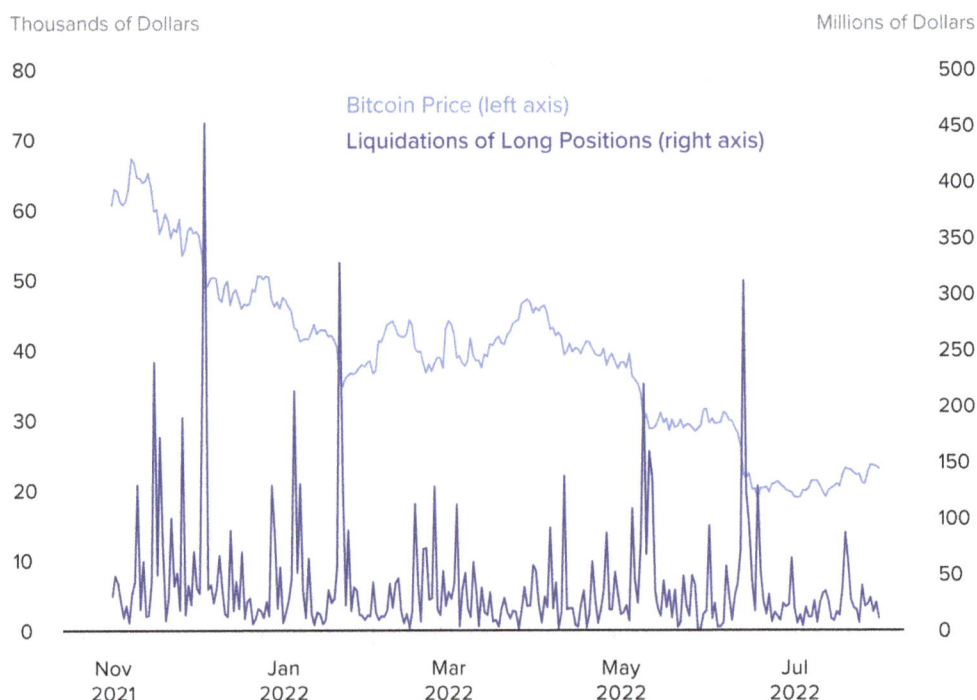

Source: Coinalyze

Notes: The liquidations data aggregate liquidations of long Bitcoin positions across contracts at selected crypto-asset trading platforms, converted to US dollars.

133 Joseph Young, "How massive liquidations caused Bitcoin to plummet 16% in 24 hours," CoinTelegraph, November 26, 2020, at https://cointelegraph.com/news/how-massive-liquidations-caused-bitcoin-to-plummet-16-in-24-hours/.

134 Ben McKenzie and Jacob Silverman, "Why users are pushing back against the world's largest crypto exchange," *The Washington Post*, April 1, 2022, at https://www.washingtonpost.com/outlook/2022/04/01/binance-may-19-lawsuit-cryptocurrency/.

Leverage at Crypto-Asset Platforms

Crypto-asset platforms provide leverage to their customers through several products, including margin loans or collateralized loans, futures, other derivatives, and "leveraged tokens." The availability of these products to U.S. investors may be more limited than to investors overseas, though some platforms, including platforms based overseas or platforms that are promoted as "decentralized," reportedly do not rigorously enforce geographic restrictions.[135] In the United States, platforms offering leverage through margin loans or derivatives contracts to U.S. investors, even if located overseas or purportedly "decentralized," must comply with U.S. rules and regulations, including those that have the effect of putting safeguards on the amounts of leverage available as well as providing for more comprehensive regulation and oversight of the market for these products. Part 4, Regulation of Crypto-Asset Activities, provides more detail on U.S. regulations that apply to leverage. As currently operating, market participants may be in non-compliance with applicable laws and regulations and, therefore, adherence to leverage safeguards is unlikely.

Platforms do not generally make available statistics on the average or actual amount of leverage that customers avail themselves of in practice. Therefore, it remains fairly unclear how many market participants use leverage provided by platforms, the size of their positions, or the frequency of margin calls and liquidations. However, some information on available leverage can be gleaned from news media reports or from advertisements or announcements on platforms' websites. In general, products that provide high leverage on overseas crypto-asset platforms are reportedly very popular. For example, perpetual futures contracts (those which have no expiry or settlement dates) reportedly have very large volumes of activity on overseas crypto-asset platforms, especially in Bitcoin and other assets with the deepest and most liquid markets. Overall, the volume of futures trading at large platforms appears to have grown substantially based on the popularity of certain futures products with high leverage.

Large overseas platforms advertise extraordinarily high levels of leverage on some perpetual futures contracts, including as high as 125x leverage on specific contracts, though they generally claim not to make such contracts available to U.S. customers.[136] Some platforms that describe themselves as "decentralized" may also offer similarly high leverage on specific contracts. Perpetual futures contracts are popular in crypto-asset markets for the purposes of speculation or hedging because they are settled in cash rather than in delivery of the crypto-asset, and because they do not have expiry or settlement dates. At leverage levels up to 125x, even a relatively

---

135 Alexander Osipovich, "U.S. Crypto Traders Evade Offshore Exchange Bans," *The Wall Street Journal*, July 30, 2021, at https://www.wsj.com/articles/u-s-crypto-traders-evade-offshore-exchange-bans-11627637401.

136 Sirio Aramonte, Wenqian Huang, and Andreas Schrimpf, "DeFi risks and the Decentralisation Illusion," BIS, December 2021, at https://www.bis.org/publ/qtrpdf/r_qt2112b.pdf.

modest adverse price move could result in the position going underwater, resulting in a potentially significant loss to the position that had to be liquidated. In the U.S., platforms appear to offer leverage as high as 10x on certain products and continue to add leveraged products geared to retail investors to their offerings.[137]

Margin loans appear to be commonly offered by U.S.-based platforms, often with maximum borrowing capacity capped at 50 percent of the value of the collateral. In general, perpetual futures and collateralized loans may have similar attributes in crypto-asset markets. Leverage in crypto-asset markets generally relies on pre-funded collateral rather than on margin calls. Platforms typically use some level of collateral and then rely on auto-liquidations of that collateral when a position's value falls below some margin maintenance level.

Overseas platforms also offer crypto-assets known as "leveraged tokens" that provide lower levels of leverage than perpetuals, reportedly between 1.25x and 4x leverage. Leveraged tokens are designed to provide leveraged exposure to an underlying crypto-asset, for example, by referencing a basket of futures contracts. Some market participants may prefer such crypto-assets to futures contracts because they can avoid the potential for liquidation associated with futures contracts, even if lower leverage is available. Leveraged tokens achieve this feature by rebalancing periodically or after reaching certain thresholds to maintain a targeted amount of leverage.

Some platforms are described by their promoters as decentralized, or as DeFi protocols. DeFi protocols facilitate or incentivize a range of activities, including the borrowing of one crypto-asset using another as collateral, and transactions that have similarities to derivative products. Much DeFi activity appears to entail the use of leverage, and so the overall volume of activity on DeFi protocols can provide some broad perspective on the use of leverage, as measured by the total value locked in DeFi protocols. Though these data on total valued locked are unverified, this measure indicates that DeFi activity grew substantially during 2021, along with the associated use of leverage, as shown in **Figure 13**. However, in 2022, the total value locked on DeFi protocols has substantially declined, in line with declines in broad crypto-asset market sentiment and prices. **Figure 14** shows this decline in reported DeFi Total Value Locked has taken place across activity categories.

---

137 FTX.US, "Spot Margin Trading," at https://help.ftx.us/hc/en-us/articles/360046850054-Spot-Margin-Trading. Coinbase, "Coinbase Derivatives Exchange to make nano bitcoin futures available through leading brokers," June 23, 2022, at https://blog.coinbase.com/coinbase-derivatives-exchange-to-make-nano-bitcoin-futures-available-through-leading-brokers-8df2582325da.

Figure 13: Reported Total Value Locked, By Blockchain

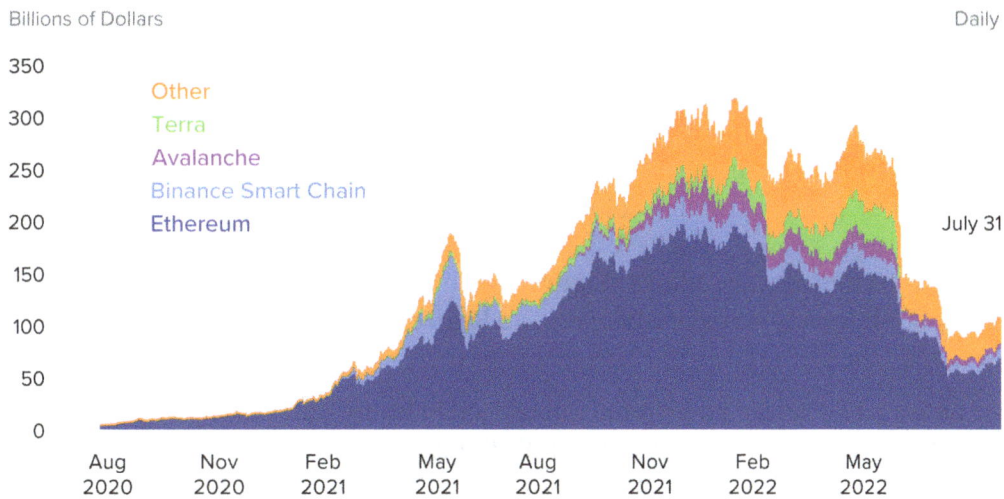

Billions of Dollars   Daily

Other
Terra
Avalanche
Binance Smart Chain
Ethereum
                                                                  July 31

Source: DeFiLlama

Notes: Total Value Locked is the overall value of assets committed to a DeFi protocol. This metric includes governance tokens staked in the protocol, staked liquidity provider tokens where one of the coins in the pair is the governance token, and borrowed coins in lending protocols.

Figure 14: Reported Total Value Locked, By Category

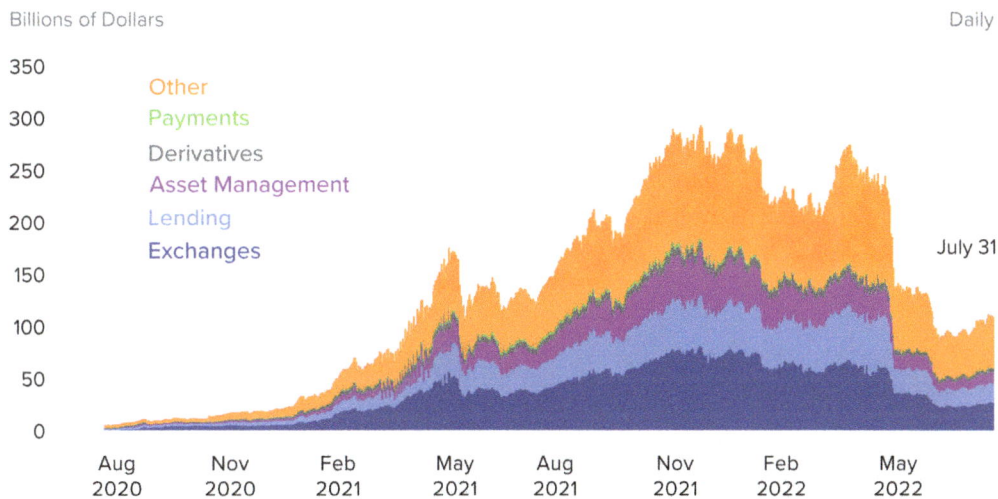

Billions of Dollars   Daily

Other
Payments
Derivatives
Asset Management
Lending
Exchanges
                                                                  July 31

Source: DeFiLlama

Notes: Total Value Locked is the overall value of assets committed to a DeFi protocol. This metric includes governance tokens staked in the protocol, staked liquidity provider tokens where one of the coins in the pair is the governance token, and borrowed crypto-assets in lending protocols. Certain crypto-assets are double counted across protocols.

Leverage at CFTC-registered Exchanges

A second source of leverage comes from futures on crypto-assets and options on crypto-asset futures listed by CFTC-registered exchanges involving some traditional financial institutions. For example, futures on Bitcoin and Ether, and options on Bitcoin and Ether futures, are available for trading on the Chicago Mercantile Exchange (CME), among others. The CME Bitcoin futures product has seen significant increases in trading volume and open interest over the last several years. Some crypto-asset platforms have also established CFTC-registered exchanges with crypto-asset derivative products. **Figure 15** shows open interest in CFTC-regulated Bitcoin/USD futures across exchanges, and **Figure 16** shows open interest in CFTC-regulated Ether/USD futures across exchanges.

The amount of leverage an investor can take on in futures contracts traded on CFTC-registered exchanges is generally limited by the rules of the exchanges, clearinghouses, and intermediaries involved in the transactions. The margin requirements set forth by exchanges, clearinghouses, and intermediaries are also subject to CFTC oversight. Currently, CME initial margin requirements allow for 2x leverage for Bitcoin futures and 1.67x leverage for Ether futures. Clearinghouses, and intermediaries such as futures commission merchants (FCMs), have the discretion to impose higher margin requirements on customers than the exchange margin requirements, resulting in less leverage available to the customers.[138] Investors may also obtain leverage through the use of margin in holdings of Bitcoin futures ETFs. Securities margin requirements generally permit 2x leverage.

---

138 *See, e.g.,* https://www.cmegroup.com/markets/cryptocurrencies/bitcoin/bitcoin.margins.html and https://www.cmegroup.com/markets/cryptocurrencies/ether/ether.margins.html, accessed January 2022. The margin levels for CME Bitcoin futures are set at around 35% of the notional amount of the contract, thus providing for almost 3x leverage, according to Alex Ferko, Amani Moin, Esen Onur, and Miachael Penick, "Who Trades Bitcoin Futures and Why?" Working Paper, November 4, 2021, at https://www.cftc.gov/sites/default/files/2021-11/WhoTradesBTC_V2_ada.pdf.

Figure 15: Open Interest of CFTC-Regulated Bitcoin/USD Futures

Futures Open Interest
(in Coin Equivalents)

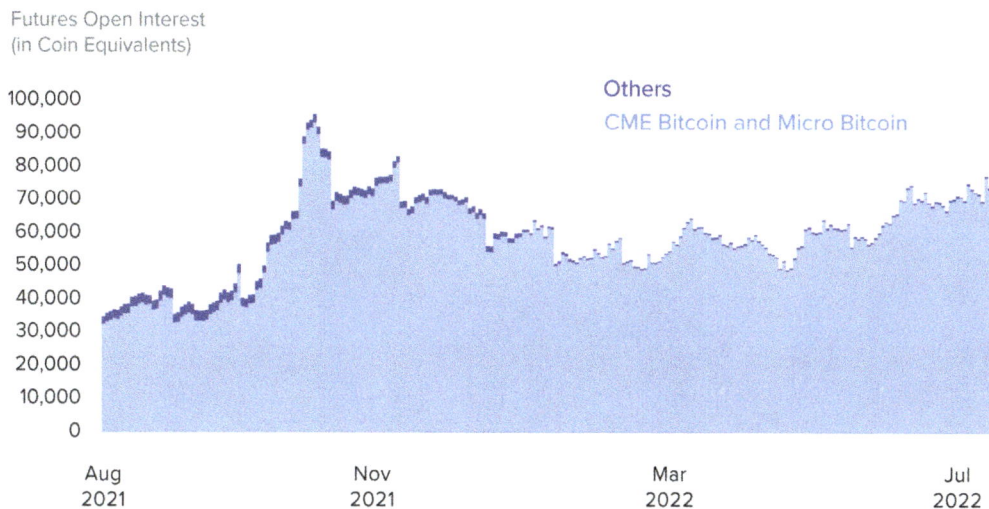

Source: CFTC

Notes: Normalized Open Interest of Bitcoin/USD pair futures contracts; open interest adjusted for each listed contract's respective size/multiplier and represents coin equivalent figures. Other contracts include ICE Bakkt Bitcoin USD monthly, Bitnomial Bitcoin USD, ERISX Bounded Bitcoin, Coinbase / FAIRX Nano Bitcoin, LedgerX/FTX Bitcoin.

Figure 16: Open Interest of CFTC-Regulated Ether/USD Futures

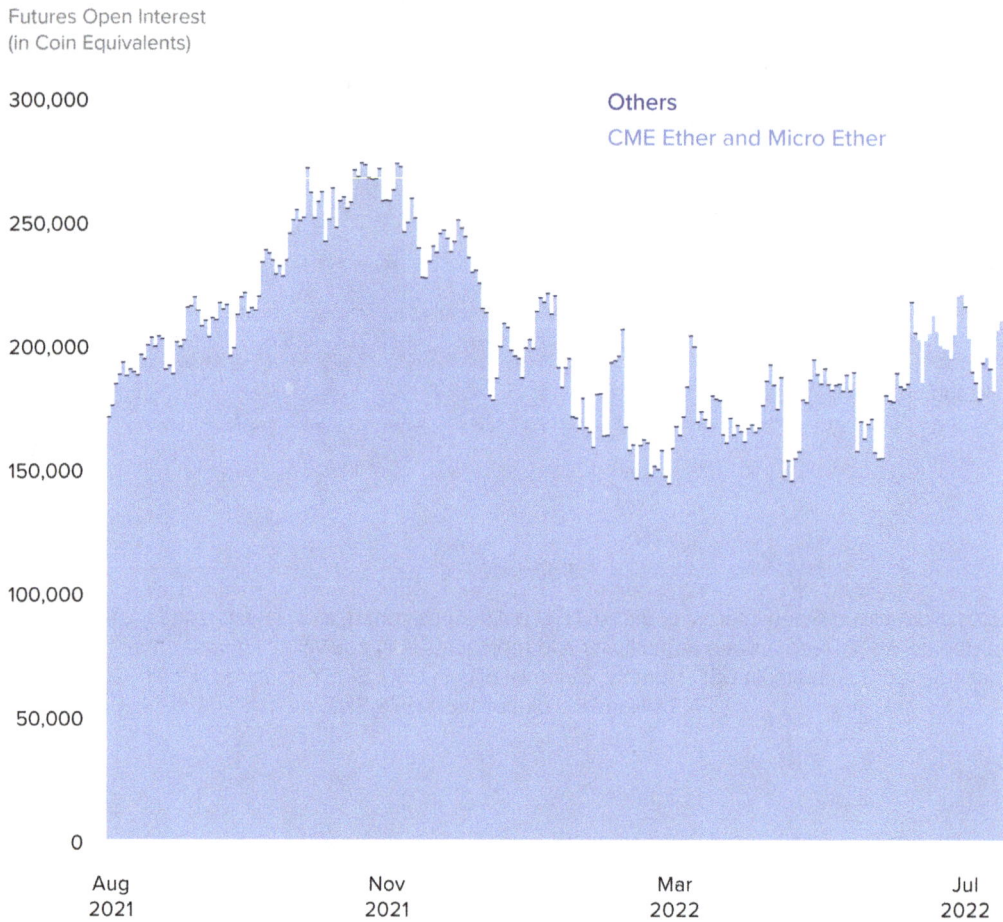

Futures Open Interest
(in Coin Equivalents)

Others

CME Ether and Micro Ether

Source: CFTC

Notes: Normalized Open Interest of Ether/USD pair futures contracts; open interest adjusted for each listed contract's respective size/multiplier and represents coin equivalent figures. Others include ERISX Bounded Ether, LedgerX/FTX Ethereum.

Prime Brokerage-type Services

A third source of leverage is the collection of prime brokerage-type services that are emerging in the crypto-assets markets. Several large crypto-assets platforms reportedly offer prime brokerage-type services aimed at high-net-worth individuals, wealth managers, hedge funds, and other institutional investors. While it is possible that traditional U.S. financial institutions may be offering prime brokerage-type services to their hedge fund clients engaged in crypto-asset activities, there is little information available about such activities and little indication that such activity is significant at this time.

Prime brokerage activity in crypto-asset markets may be poised to grow rapidly. Some of the prime brokerage risks that exist in traditional finance could also be present in crypto-asset markets. So far, traditional institutional investors who have entered the crypto-assets space have reportedly focused on gaining long exposure to relatively more established crypto-assets such as Bitcoin. But as these institutions begin to seek out ways to enhance the returns of their crypto-assets holdings, they may look to prime brokerage providers for financing solutions such as lending and borrowing of crypto-assets, facilitating leverage through synthetic exposure to the underlying crypto-assets, and providing access to different financial products and more complex and leveraged trading strategies.

Loans to Miners

Finally, a different kind of leverage present in the crypto-asset ecosystem involves crypto-asset miners that finance their operations by taking out loans collateralized against their mining equipment. Such loans reportedly totaled up to $4 billion in June 2022.[139] Since the value of the mining equipment tends to be a function of the price of crypto-assets to be mined, falling crypto-asset prices also put pressure on the value of mining equipment collateralizing these loans. If miners were to conduct fire sales of mining equipment in order to meet payments associated with these loans, a downward spiral of prices could result if sales of mining equipment were to put further downward pressure on prices by making it cheaper to mine. In addition, some miners have reportedly sold Bitcoin to help cover operational costs or pay down loans, putting further downward pressure on Bitcoin prices. The value of mining equipment may also be affected by developments in the energy market.

Liquidation Practices

The method of liquidating leveraged positions can have substantial implications for whether the unwinding of those positions affects orderly market conditions. Automated liquidation, combined with high leverage, potentially heightens financial stability risks, though alternative forms of liquidation also may create financial stability risks. In light of the high price volatility associated with most crypto-assets, perpetual futures contracts tied to those assets that allow for very high levels of leverage are likely subject to automated liquidation in short time periods. Collateralized loans are subject to margin calls if the value of the collateral decreases, and borrowers' collateral may be liquidated if margin calls are not met or if loans are not repaid.

Automated liquidations without appropriate regulatory guardrails are likely procyclical, exacerbating balance sheet distress at a time of falling asset values and potentially creating a cascade of automated liquidations. Compared to alternative

---

139 David Pan, "Almost $4 Billion in Bitcoin Miner Loans Are Coming Under Stress," *Bloomberg*, June 24, 2022, at https://www.bloomberg.com/news/articles/2022-06-24/almost-4-billion-in-bitcoin-miner-loans-are-coming-under-stress?sref=PHkj6DsL.

liquidation mechanisms, automated liquidation may cause lenders to be more likely to liquidate. While lenders may also be likely to liquidate earlier to avoid losses, frequent and early liquidation may put downward pressure on crypto-asset prices by reacting to temporary price changes during small windows of time. The limited, or nonexistent, capacity for human intervention to prevent liquidation governed by smart contracts poses particular risks that standard tools would be unavailable to address crypto-asset market stress, for example through adjustments to margin requirements or trading stoppages. However, it is not clear how often platforms rely on automated liquidations or how those liquidations work in practice. In addition, platforms may have other strategies to govern the resolution of leveraged positions, including backstop liquidity providers or insurance funds.

Interaction of automated liquidation using oracles to provide off-chain inputs creates the possibility that oracles may feed data in unexpected ways, leading to potentially unnecessary automatic liquidations. Oracles may be subject to manipulation, attacks, or timing mismatches. Other timing issues could also lead market participants that use leverage to inadvertently take on riskier-than-desired trading positions. For example, if a market participant were to hedge a short position in a spot market with the use of a crypto-asset derivative, automated liquidation of that derivative would cause the participant's position to become unhedged. Such liquidations could take place overnight when traditional financial markets are closed, creating settlement timing mismatches even if the short position was closed out once traditional financial markets opened the next day. An additional element of automated liquidation is the role of liquidation bots, which are managed by third parties and able to identify and then move to liquidate undercollateralized positions.

Automated liquidation may interact with vulnerabilities created by counterparties with significant interconnections. In DeFi protocols, automated liquidation may limit the available tools for resolving large positions in an orderly manner. For example, in June 2022, the prospective liquidation of a single large margin position on a DeFi protocol on the Solana blockchain reportedly raised concerns that such a liquidation could cause a "meltdown" of the protocol.[140] In some instances, participants in DeFi protocols have reportedly taken steps to avoid automated liquidations of large positions that could result in disorderly trading conditions. Even though these DeFi arrangements are nominally decentralized, in practice a core group of promoters with concentrated control of purported "governance" tokens have in some instances used governance votes in an attempt to address large positions or other issues. For instance, in the example from June 2022, a governance vote reportedly granted a group known as Solend Labs the ability to liquidate their position through over-the-counter trades, though that vote was later

---

140 Ezra Reguerra, "Solend invalidates Solana whale wallet takeover plan with second governance vote," *Coin Telegraph*, June 20, 2022, at https://cointelegraph.com/news/solend-invalidates-solana-whale-wallet-takeover-plan-with-second-governance-vote.

nullified by a second vote.[141] Around the same time, several other DeFi protocols reportedly adjusted their practices and policies to reduce the likelihood of large-scale liquidations.[142] As another example, in November 2021, participants in the "Emergency DAO" of a DeFi platform acted to shut down a liquidity pool through which participants had acquired a large amount of voting power in that DeFi protocol's governance system.[143]

Liquidation can also involve a liquidation fee. Liquidation is typically governed by a collateralization ratio, sometimes called a "health factor." If a limit on that measure is breached, borrowers' loans can be liquidated and a portion of their collateral can be seized, inclusive of a liquidation fee. This liquidation fee is sometimes called a "liquidation bonus" for the liquidator, or a "liquidation penalty" for the borrower, and is taken out of the value of the collateral upon liquidation. These liquidation fees are often not disclosed to the user at the point of borrowing, but may instead be listed in the FAQs or protocol documentation.[144]

Rehypothecation

Leverage in crypto-asset markets sometimes involves the practice of rehypothecation, which can generate additional leverage by reusing the same collateral to secure multiple instances of leverage. For example, a crypto-asset platform might make a loan backed by crypto-assets, such as stablecoins, and the platform might then secure a loan using the posted collateral.[145] Platforms that engage in this type of activity may have large risk exposures as a result. The extent of this activity is obscured by lack of adequate disclosure about rehypothecation, raising serious risk that vulnerabilities could build up unseen. Because rehypothecation appears to commonly involve stablecoins, leverage may interact with the other vulnerabilities posed by stablecoins, including run risk.

---

141 Ezra Reguerra, "Solend invalidates Solana whale wallet takeover plan with second governance vote," *Coin Telegraph*, June 20, 2022, at https://cointelegraph.com/news/solend-invalidates-solana-whale-wallet-takeover-plan-with-second-governance-vote.

142 Olga Kharif, "Mounting Crypto Liquidations Make DeFi Go to Extremes" *Bloomberg*, June 19, 2022, at https://www.bloomberg.com/news/articles/2022-06-19/mounting-crypto-liquidation-risks-cause-defi-to-go-to-extremes.

143 Andrew Thurman, "'Curve Wars' Heat Up: Emergency DAO Invoked After 'Clear Governance Attack,'" *CoinDesk*, November 11, 2021, at https://www.coindesk.com/business/2021/11/11/curve-wars-heat-up-emergency-dao-invoked-after-clear-governance-attack/.

144 Testimony of Alexis Goldstein before the Joint Economic Committee, US Congress, November 17, 2021, at https://www.jec.senate.gov/public/_cache/files/aa387917-9456-4b1f-a948-f086594c4d15/alexis-goldstein-jec-crypto-hearing-testimony.pdf.

145 Eliot Brown and Caitlin Ostroff, "Behind the Celsius Sales Pitch Was a Crypto Firm Built on Risk," *The Wall Street Journal*, June 30, 2022, at https://www.wsj.com/articles/behind-the-celsius-sales-pitch-was-a-crypto-firm-built-on-risk-11656498142.

Borrowing Spirals

DeFi lending protocols may encourage participation by borrowers by distributing new crypto-assets to users. For example, a market participant might invest a stablecoin in a DeFi protocol and be compensated in part based on the issuance of a "governance token," which can then be invested in another protocol and earn another return, creating what is known as a "borrowing spiral." Such spirals may create heightened risk of abrupt liquidation for market participants, as the entire chain of leveraged positions could be unwound if any link were to be forced into liquidation. Though such arrangements create liquidity for a time, that liquidity can evaporate quickly if these leveraged positions are unwound, and operational issues can arise in the event of abrupt unwinding.

Underwriting

The underwriting of leveraged positions appears to be fairly weak compared to underwriting in the traditional financial sector. Crypto-asset market underwriting generally focuses solely on collateralization. Since credit checks appear to be uncommon, market participants may have large exposures to counterparties with a history of reckless financial actions, or whose identities are unclear, making those relationships riskier than measured by the collateral itself. In general, borrowers and lenders may have severely misaligned incentives. Legal questions regarding the ability to perfect liens against crypto-assets and foreclose on those assets also increase risks. Lending to DeFi protocols further complicates risk management considerations. Dispensing with considerations of counterparty credit risk raises concerns that such risks may build up unseen. Because these activities may not provide recourse other than to the crypto-asset, the potential for price manipulation of the crypto-asset creates additional risk.

Finally, many crypto-asset activities provide access to leverage for retail investors with limited due diligence or risk assessments, especially in comparison to other markets.

3.4 Interactions Among the Vulnerabilities

Each of the vulnerabilities discussed to this point can operate independently. However, interactions among the vulnerabilities are quite likely, and more generally, crypto-asset markets show evidence of common procyclicality in which several vulnerabilities build simultaneously and interactively. For example, leverage may help fuel speculative activity and drive up crypto-asset prices. In turn, high prices may induce market participants to take on more leverage. In a market downturn, asset price declines may be reinforced by automated liquidations of leveraged positions, and the potential for cascading liquidations may make significant drops in prices particularly likely.

As another example, if a platform is also an issuer of a stablecoin, lower demand for the services of the platform may result in lower demand for the stablecoins it issues and lead to redemptions. That can cause forced selling and exacerbate risks to the traditional financial system.

Furthermore, crypto-asset markets are rapidly evolving. As new developments occur, they could create new vulnerabilities. For instance, stablecoins developed as a way to facilitate other market interactions such as trading of crypto-assets or DeFi activities. In the process, stablecoins facilitated the growth of vulnerabilities associated with those activities, introducing interconnections, and run risks related to the stablecoin issuers. As an illustration, Box B discusses how the collapse of the TerraUSD stablecoin led to losses for investors in that project, which reportedly included firms involved in proprietary trading, investment funds, and venture capital. The run also disrupted DeFi arrangements that were built on the Terra blockchain.[146]

3.5 Risks of Scale

Though the scale of crypto-asset activities is currently relatively small compared to the size of the overall U.S. financial system, they could scale quickly. Since vulnerabilities inside the crypto-asset ecosystem are acute, the financial stability risks of crypto-assets would be substantial if those vulnerabilities were to remain in place while the scale of crypto-asset activities and interconnectedness with the traditional financial system were to grow rapidly.

The path to attaining large scale carries its own risks and challenges.[147] Scale might involve network effects, for example, if one blockchain, protocol, stablecoin, or other crypto-asset were to become dominant and foster rapid growth. Such dominance could lead to concentration risks, and market participants would likely suffer losses associated with the blockchains, protocols, or assets, that, in this scenario, did not become dominant. Scale may be achieved quickly if platforms introduce new products and services and build network effects for users, for example. The PWG Report discussed risks related to the concentration of economic power and stablecoins.[148] Greater scale could also intensify the pace and scope of cybersecurity shocks, as crypto-assets would be increasingly tempting targets, particularly given

---

146 "The Collapse of Anchor," Greythorn Asset Management, June 8, 2022, at https://www.greythorn.com/the-collapse-of-anchor.

147 For further discussion, see BIS, "The Future Monetary System," *Annual Economic Report 2022*, June 21, 2022, at https://www.bis.org/publ/arpdf/ar2022e3.htm#crypto.

148 PWG, FDIC, and OCC, *Report on Stablecoins*, November 2021, p. 14, https://home.treasury.gov/system/files/136/StableCoinReport_Nov1_508.pdf.

the heightened cybersecurity risks of these activities. Greater scale may also cause large changes in wealth of certain market participants.[149]

Financial stability risks of scale are distinct from, but related to, a set of technological challenges often referred to as the "scalability problem," which refers to the throughput limitations of crypto-asset technology in processing large amounts of transactions.[150] The attention given to this problem is itself a sign of the great interest among industry participants in increasing the scale of crypto-asset activities. While proposed innovations that address scalability achieve higher throughput, they may also contribute to financial stability risks. For example, if greater scale is achieved through greater centralization, very large entities may directly pose financial stability risks. Such entities might own large amounts of assets that, if liquidated, could substantially weigh on key financial markets, for example. Alternatively, attaining large scale with a large degree of decentralization may reduce opportunities for intervention in the event of a panic.[151]

So-called "layer 2" solutions are developing as a means of increasing transaction output.[152] However, layer 2 solutions decrease the transparency of crypto-asset activities, reducing the ability for market participants and regulators to monitor the buildup of financial stability vulnerabilities such as interconnections.

In addition, at scale, many additional policy issues beyond financial stability could gain prominence. These include:

- issues related to investor and consumer protection and market integrity, discussed in Box E and in more detail by United States Department of the Treasury, *Crypto-Assets: Implications for Consumers, Investors, and Businesses*;[153]
- illicit financing risks and risks to national security, discussed in more detail by United States Department of the Treasury, *Action Plan to Address Illicit Financing Risks of Digital Assets*;[154]
- risks to international monetary and payment system integrity;
- macro-financial risks including monetary policy transmission, disintermediation of existing financial institutions, and international capital flows;

---

149 Financial Stability Board, "Assessment of Risks to Financial Stability from Crypto-assets," February 16, 2022, at https://www.fsb.org/2022/02/fsb-warns-of-emerging-risks-from-crypto-assets-to-global-financial-stability/.

150 MIT Digital Currency Initiative, "Scalability," at https://dci.mit.edu/scalability.

151 *See, for example,* Hilary Allen, "$=€=Bitcoin?" Maryland Law Review, vol. 76, p. 877, 2017, at https://papers.ssrn.com/sol3/papers.cfm?abstract_id=2645001.

152 Kevin Dwyer, "What are Cryptocurrency Layer 2 Scaling Solutions?" Coin Market Cap, at https://coinmarketcap.com/alexandria/article/what-are-cryptocurrency-layer-2-scaling-solutions.

153 https://home.treasury.gov/system/files/136/CryptoAsset_EO5.pdf

154 https://home.treasury.gov/system/files/136/Digital-Asset-Action-Plan.pdf

- energy security risks, given the energy needed for crypto-asset activities;
- and the climate-related financial risks that could arise related to the climate impact of crypto-asset mining.

3.6 Sources of Shocks

Shocks are inherently difficult to predict or describe in advance. In addition, even when shocks materialize, pinpointing the exact cause can be challenging. For example, the cause of the rout in crypto-asset prices during the spring of 2022 can be difficult to precisely identify, though changes in investor sentiment may have been related to changes in the macroeconomic landscape and the prospect of higher inflation and higher nominal yields on other assets. Nevertheless, some key features of crypto-asset activities suggest that certain sources of shocks may be likely.

Malicious Acts

First, shocks from malicious actors are likely. Malicious acts include numerous instances of fraud, discussed in more detail in part 3.3.1, Crypto-Asset Prices. Malicious acts also include theft or misappropriation. Attributes of crypto-asset activities may make them prone to attacks. The relative immutability of many crypto-asset activities may prevent a malicious transaction from being reversed. The heavily technological nature of these activities may provide a number of potential weak points for malicious actors to target. By the nature of DLT, code underlying crypto-asset activities is both open for review publicly and is generally difficult to change. As a result, other market participants have little ability to quickly prevent such attacks or implement cybersecurity options. The perceived anonymity or pseudonymous nature of crypto-asset activities has provided malicious actors with some ability to escape identification. In addition, malicious actors have access to a number of obfuscation techniques that enable crypto-asset flows to be hidden or obscured. Such techniques include but are not limited to cross-chain hopping, utilizing opaque "Layer 2" protocols, the use of mixers and tumblers, and converting one crypto-asset to an anonymity-enhanced crypto-asset, also known as "privacy coins."[155] Finally, despite the general transparency of DLT, vulnerabilities may be difficult to identify. A software bill of materials (SBOM), which is used to record the

---

155 FinCEN, "Financial Trend Analysis," October 2021, at https://www.fincen.gov/sites/default/files/2021-10/Financial%20Trend%20Analysis_Ransomware%20508%20FINAL.pdf.

details and provenance of software, may make operational risks more apparent to users.[156]

Public reports suggest that crypto-asset activities have been the subject of many malicious attacks that exemplify the potential for shocks. That said, the exact extent of such attacks is hard to measure since these events are typically opaque and not subject to public audits or disclosures. **Figure 17** shows one estimate of the volume of funds stolen via DeFi hacks over time.

Figure 17: Estimated Volume of Funds Stolen via DeFi Hacks

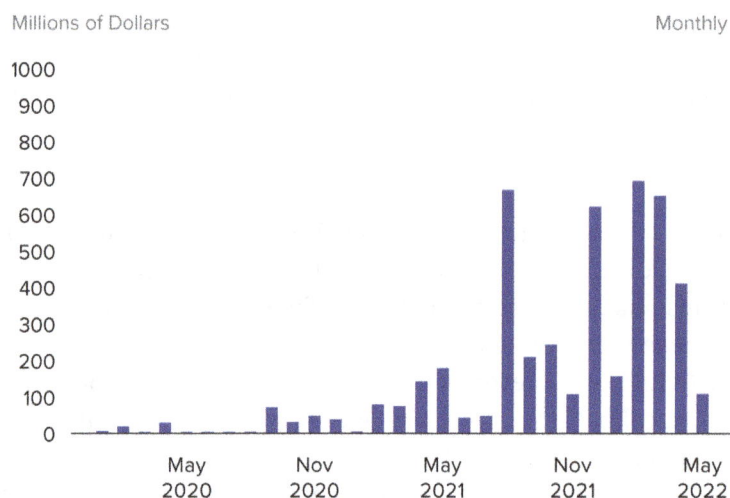

Source: Rekt.news, staff calculations

The proceeds of such attacks are measured in dollars at the time of the attacks, and the dollar value of such proceeds fluctuates in value over time. **Figure 18** shows that

---

156 "[T]he term 'Software Bill of Materials' or 'SBOM' means a formal record containing the details and supply chain relationships of various components used in building software. Software developers and vendors often create products by assembling existing open source and commercial software components. The SBOM enumerates these components in a product. It is analogous to a list of ingredients on food packaging. An SBOM is useful to those who develop or manufacture software, those who select or purchase software, and those who operate software. Developers often use available open source and third-party software components to create a product; an SBOM allows the builder to make sure those components are up to date and to respond quickly to new vulnerabilities. Buyers can use an SBOM to perform vulnerability or license analysis, both of which can be used to evaluate risk in a product. Those who operate software can use SBOMs to quickly and easily determine whether they are at potential risk of a newly discovered vulnerability. A widely used, machine-readable SBOM format allows for greater benefits through automation and tool integration. The SBOMs gain greater value when collectively stored in a repository that can be easily queried by other applications and systems. Understanding the supply chain of software, obtaining an SBOM, and using it to analyze known vulnerabilities are crucial in managing risk." Exec. Order No. 14028, 86 Fed. Reg. 26633, 26646 (May 17, 2022), at https://www.govinfo.gov/content/pkg/FR-2021-05-17/pdf/2021-10460.pdf.

attack proceeds vary with the price of Bitcoin, likely indicating a combination of two factors: higher-valued assets are more tempting targets, and that the proceeds of any attack will be higher in value when asset prices are high.

Figure 18: Bitcoin Prices and 30-day Moving Average of Total Value Received by Crypto-Asset Scams

Source: Chainalysis

Note: the historic estimated volume of scams may change in the future as further research uncovers additional scams that took place.

Shocks could arise from acts of fraud, as discussed in part 3.3.1, Crypto-Asset Prices, and Box E. Shocks could also arise from malicious cyber security attacks, including state-sponsored attacks. For example, the FBI announced that hackers affiliated with North Korea (the LAZARUS Group) were responsible for the approximately $620 million hack of the Ronin network.[157] Such hacks can create substantial losses for market participants, and financial stability impacts would be particularly likely if a hack disrupted the operations of a large entity that has considerable interconnections or provides a key service.

Attacks could also take the form of hacks, coding exploits, and novel forms of attacks such as a flash loan attack, 51 percent attacks to manipulate governance mechanisms, malicious acts associated with forks, and airdrop phishing. As an

---

157 Federal Bureau of Investigation, "FBI Statement on Attribution of Malicious Cyber Activity Posed by the Democratic People's Republic of Korea," April 14, 2022, at https://www.fbi.gov/news/press-releases/press-releases/fbi-statement-on-attribution-of-malicious-cyber-activity-posed-by-the-democratic-peoples-republic-of-korea.

example of a governance mechanism attack, malicious actors organized an attack on the Beanstalk stablecoin in which attackers used a large flash loan to purchase a majority of the stablecoin's governance tokens. The attackers then rapidly used an emergency governance mechanism to vote to transfer the stablecoin's reserves to a private wallet held by the attackers. This enabled the malicious actors to pay off the flash loan instantaneously and pocket the remainder of the funds.[158]

Cross-chain bridges have been a common target of malicious attacks, highlighting the risks created by attempts at increasing inter-operability of crypto-asset activities. One report estimates that $2 billion in crypto-assets was stolen from cross-chain bridges during the first seven months of 2022.[159] These attacks[160] have included theft of:

- $611 million of crypto-assets in August 2021 from the Poly Network;
- $620 million of crypto-assets from the Ronin bridge (as noted above);
- $325 million of crypto-assets from the Wormhole bridge between Solana and Ethereum;
- $190 million of crypto-assets in August 2022 from the Nomad bridge by multiple users following the discovery of a fatal security flaw;
- And $100 million from the Horizon bridge between the Harmony and Ethereum and Binance Smart Chain blockchains.

Attacks have targeted many other crypto-asset activities. For example:

- attacks have also targeted oracles, including a $13.4 million theft in April 2022 from Deus Dao;
- users lost $120 million in crypto-assets when the BadgerDAO User Interface (UI) was hacked in December 2021;
- a security breach of the wallets of the platform BitMart in December 2021 led to a $196 million loss; and
- a coding vulnerability at the DeFi protocol Compound led to a $147 million loss in September 2021.

Recent reports have suggested that so-called "black hat" hackers have recently shifted their focus to crypto-asset markets, particularly DeFi protocols.[161]

---

158 In a flash loan, the loan and its subsequent repayment are recorded in a single block of a blockchain, resolving the position at the same time it is created. Alex Hern, "Beanstalk cryptocurrency loses $182m of reserves in flash 'attack'" *The Guardian*, April 18, 2022, at https://www.theguardian.com/technology/2022/apr/18/beanstalk-cryptocurrency-loses-182m-of-reserves-in-flash-attack.

159 Chainalysis, "Vulnerabilities in Cross-chain Bridge Protocols Emerge as Top Security Risk," August 2, 2022, at https://blog.chainalysis.com/reports/cross-chain-bridge-hacks-2022/.

160 *See* rekt.news for descriptions of these episodes.

161 Ruholamin Haqshanas, "Hackers Stole USD 670M from DeFi Projects in Q2, Up by 50% from Q2 2021," Crypto News, July 6, 2022, at https://cryptonews.com/news/hackers-stole-usd-670m-from-defi-projects-in-q2-up-by-50-from-q-2021.htm.

Technology Breakdowns

Another source of shocks could arise from the heavy reliance of crypto-assets on technology, and the novelty and complexity of that technology. Non-malicious coding issues that pose a risk include bugs, unexpected problems created by publicly available code, or failed protocol updates. The reliance on communications technology may result in shocks from potential internet outages or other failures and crashes related to technology. Finally, a large set of shocks may arise from non-malicious technology-related security breaches, including the loss or theft of private keys and related cold storage risks, disruptions to off-chain transactions, and a broad set of potential problems related to encryption or failure of encryption. For example, loss of private keys by a custody platform was alleged by a lawsuit in June 2021, involving a $75 million loss.[162]

Governance or Decision-making Breakdowns

Another source of shocks could be governance or decision-making breakdowns. Some management functions in crypto-asset activities may also be programmatic by nature, in which case the capacity for human intervention during a crisis depends on "governance votes" to alter code. Breakdowns could arise in the execution of these mechanisms, especially those that feature fragmentation or decentralization. Solutions to decision-making problems may require the agreement by some set of "governance" token holders, miners, validators, node operators, and others.[163] Paralysis could result from a failure to reach an agreement. Alternatively, governance arrangements are also vulnerable to 51 percent attacks, in which malicious actors acquire a slim majority of governance voting tokens.[164]

Governance arrangements may also create poor incentives and result in poor decision-making. Voting rights holders may lack expertise, time, interest, or fitness to fulfill any meaningful oversight role. The incentives of voting right holders may not be well aligned with users, and collective decision making is always difficult in the presence of diverging interests. For example, developers may hold a large share of voting rights and their interests may not be well aligned with market participants. Indeed, according to one report, many crypto-asset governance tokens are held by the top 1 percent of holders of a given token, creating the potential for the largest

---

162 Meir Orbach, "Crypto-assets Security Company Fireblocks Sued for Losing $75 Million Worth of ETH," *CTECH*, June 21, 2021, at https://www.calcalistech.com/ctech/articles/0,7340,L-3910671,00.html.

163 IOSCO, "IOSCO Decentralized Finance Report," p. 25, March 2022, at https://www.iosco.org/library/pubdocs/pdf/IOSCOPD699.pdf.

164 Muyao Shen, "Crypto Investors Have Ignored Three Straight 51% Attacks on ETC," *CoinDesk*, September 8, 2020, at https://www.coindesk.com/markets/2020/09/08/crypto-investors-have-ignored-three-straight-51-attacks-on-etc/. Jack Martin, "Bitcoin Gold Blockchain Hit by 51% Attack Leading to $70K Double Spend," *Coin Telegraph*, January 27, 2020, at https://cointelegraph.com/news/bitcoin-gold-blockchain-hit-by-51-attack-leading-to-70k-double-spend.

holders to dominate any governance votes.[165] Market participants may not be aware of this concentration of holdings or that their interests may be misaligned with holders of significant governance tokens, in part because there may be limited disclosures of relevant information. Governance problems may be especially likely to arise if voting rights holders are anonymous or not subject to meaningful oversight or disclosure requirements.

Concentration of control may potentially subject decentralized arrangements to shocks caused by the decisions of concentrated "governance" token holders.[166] More broadly, any decision-making system that weights voting power according to the amount of a crypto-asset a user holds may distort efficient decision-making. Where consensus cannot be reached on adopting competing protocol update proposals, a crypto-asset's blockchain may fork, disrupting use of the crypto-asset and potentially leading to runs or broader investor selloffs.[167] Poorly designed governance rules can also make necessary corrections difficult.

Governance failures have arisen repeatedly, sometimes leading to the complete collapse of crypto-asset firms. For example, the unexpected and mysterious disappearance of the CEO of a crypto-asset platform, QuadrigaCX, led to the loss of $190 million and the failure of the platform, as only the CEO held the private key. Analysis by Canadian securities regulators found that QuadrigaCX was engaged in fraud.[168] Another former employee of QuadrigaCX was also discovered to be a major, but theretofore pseudonymous, developer in the DeFi protocol Wonderland, which unraveled following the news of his involvement.[169] The founder of the crypto-asset OneCoin allegedly defrauded investors of more than $4 billion before disappearing.[170]

---

165 For example, Glassnode metrics show that the top 1 percent of addresses of certain governance tokens hold over 90 percent of the total supply. https://studio.glassnode.com/metrics?a=UNI&m=distribution.Balance1PctHolders and https://studio.glassnode.com/metrics?a=COMP&m=distribution.Balance1PctHolders

166 Xiaotong Sun, Charalampos Stasinakis, and Georigios Sermpinis, "Decentralization illusion in DeFi: Evidence from MakerDAO" Working Paper, March 30, 2022, at https://arxiv.org/abs/2203.16612.

167 For example, see Adam Selene, "Crypto Market Collapse As Bitcoin Cash Fork Punishes Investors," *Crypto Briefing*, November 14, 2018, at https://cryptobriefing.com/crypto-markets-collapse-bitcoin-cash/.

168 "QuadrigaCX, A Review by Staff of the Ontario Securities Commission," April 14, 2020, at https://www.osc.gov.on.ca/quadrigacxreport/.

169 Andrew Thurman, "How Did a Former Quadriga Exec End Up Running a DeFi Protocol? Wonderland Founder Explains," *CoinDesk*, January 27, 2022, at https://www.coindesk.com/tech/2022/01/27/how-did-a-former-quadriga-exec-end-up-running-a-defi-protocol-wonderland-founder-explains/.

170 MacKenzie Sigalos, "FBI adds 'Cryptoqueen' to Ten Most Wanted Fugitives List after alleged $4 billion OneCoin fraud" *CNBC*, June 30, 2022, at https://www.cnbc.com/2022/06/30/fbi-adds-cryptoqueen-to-ten-most-wanted-fugitives-list-for-fraud.html.

Additional Sources of Shocks

This discussion is not exhaustive since, as noted, shocks are inherently unpredictable. Several other sources of shocks are also conceivable. Macroeconomic or financial developments could alter the incentives of crypto-asset investors. Shocks could arise in the traditional financial system, for example related to assets held by a stablecoin issuer. Operational disruptions could arise due to interruptions at third-party service providers, especially when the provision of services is concentrated, or in the case of electricity or internet outages. Confusion by market participants could also lead to shocks; for example, if consumers realize that products are not as regulated or insured as they had perceived or had been led to believe, or if market participants re-evaluate their views on whether certain crypto-asset activities are purportedly outside of the regulatory perimeter. Finally, different jurisdictions may take different approaches that could entail transition risks. For instance, the banning of mining by the Chinese government in 2018 appeared to put substantial downward pressure on crypto-asset prices.

4 Regulation of Crypto-Asset Activities

4.1 Overview

Robust regulation can foster stable financial market conditions by addressing and reducing financial stability vulnerabilities so that shocks are not significantly amplified. Effective regulation can also bolster confidence in market participants. Conversely, ineffective regulation can lead to unstable market conditions that could adversely impact the economy as a whole.

To date, the current regulatory framework, along with the limited overall scale of crypto-asset activities, has helped largely insulate traditional financial institutions from financial stability risks associated with crypto-assets.

The following discussion of the U.S. regulatory system for crypto-assets is structured around the set of financial stability vulnerabilities discussed in part 3, Financial Stability Risks: interconnections with the traditional financial system; crypto-asset prices; interconnections within the crypto-asset ecosystem; operational vulnerabilities; funding mismatches and risk of runs; and leverage. Each discussion covers regulations that may affect those vulnerabilities.

4.2 Regulations Relating to Interconnections with the Traditional Financial System

4.2.1 Regulation of Stablecoin Issuers' Reserve Assets

As noted in part 3.3.4, Funding Mismatches and Risk of Runs, if stablecoins were to grow rapidly without adherence to and being paired with appropriate regulation, financial stability risks could result. Regulation that addresses funding mismatches and run risk—discussed in part 4.6, Regulations Relating to Funding Mismatches and Risk of Runs—could mitigate vulnerabilities relating to interconnections with the traditional financial system through stablecoin asset holdings. That discussion notes that stablecoin issuers in the U.S. have operated under a number of different regulatory regimes, as well as outside of or in non-compliance with existing regulatory regimes. In addition, to the extent that banks hold stablecoin issuers' assets, banks are expected to account for the risks of those holdings, as discussed in part 4.2.2, Regulation of Banks', Credit Unions', and Trust Companies' Interactions with Crypto-Assets. Finally, and more generally, stablecoin issuers do not have a consistent or comprehensive regulatory framework and may engage in regulatory arbitrage, as described in part 5.3.2, Regulatory Arbitrage.

4.2.2 Regulation of Banks', Credit Unions', and Trust Companies' Interactions with Crypto-Assets

Banking Organizations[171]

Many crypto-asset companies rely on bank-provided services, as described in part 3.2, Interconnections with the Traditional Financial System. Two fundamental features of banking law govern the banking system's risks from interconnections with crypto-assets.

First, unlike most non-financial businesses that can engage in any lawful activity, banks can only engage in activities, including any crypto-asset activities, that are permissible under law and conducted in a safe and sound manner. Moreover, bank regulators may further limit a specific bank's activities, including crypto-asset activities, through conditions on charter approvals, enforcement actions, and other means. The scope of permissible activities varies based on the chartering authority–either the federal government or state governments–and the type of charter.[172] State parity or wild card laws may also provide mechanisms for state banks to engage in activities that are permissible for federally chartered banks.[173] Generally, FDIC-insured state-chartered banks and state member banks are prohibited from engaging as principal in activities that are impermissible for federally chartered banks. Finally, while bank affiliates may engage in additional activities, affiliates that are held by bank holding companies, savings and loan holding companies, and financial holding companies still face activities restrictions and are subject to federal consolidated supervision.

Second, banks also are subject to prudential oversight of their engagement in permitted activities. As with all services and activities, banks must comply with

---

171 Unless otherwise specified, "bank" refers to federally and state-chartered banks and savings associations.

172 *See, e.g.,* 12 U.S.C. §§ 24(Seventh), 92a, 1464. National banks may engage in activities that are part of or incidental to the business of banking. The business of banking is not limited to the examples specifically enumerated at 12 U.S.C. § 24(Seventh). *See NationsBank of N. Carolina, N.A. v. Variable Annuity Life Ins. Co.*, 513 U.S. 251, 258 n.2 (1995). Federal savings associations (FSAs) have authority to engage in the activities enumerated in the Home Owners' Loan Act, and in activities that are incidental to those enumerated activities. *See* 12 U.S.C. § 1464 and OTS Op. Acting Ch. Couns. (Mar. 25, 1994). In addition, Section 5A of the Home Owners' Loan Act (12 U.S.C. § 1464a), as implemented by 12 C.F.R. Part 101, authorizes FSAs with total assets of $20 billion or less, as reported to the Comptroller of the Currency as of December 31, 2017, to engage in any activity permissible for a similarly located national bank and operate as "covered savings associations."

173 Although state wild card statutes share the common goal of granting parity between state banks and national banks, these statutes vary in their reach and formulation. Most wild card statutes do not automatically grant state banks increased powers and instead require some further state action. For a discussion of state wild card and bank parity laws, see John J. Schroeder, "'Duel' Banking System? State Bank Parity Laws: An Examination of Regulatory Practice, Constitutional Issues, and Philosophical Questions," *Indiana Law Review*, vol. 36, 2003, at https://mckinneylaw.iu.edu/ilr/pdf/vol36p197.pdf.

applicable laws, including consumer protection laws, when providing crypto-asset services to customers, traditional banking services to crypto-asset entities, or otherwise engaging in crypto-asset activities. The range of prudential requirements may include capital and liquidity requirements, and proposed standards for crypto-assets are described in more detail in Box D, The Development of International Crypto-Asset Capital and Liquidity Standards for Banks. Other requirements may include affiliate and insider transaction limitations, standards related to the provision of custody and safekeeping, audit and internal control requirements, and regulatory reporting. Banks also must comply with consumer protection and anti-money laundering/combating the financing of terrorism (AML/CFT) obligations. Furthermore, banks are subject to supervision, examination, and enforcement related to these requirements.

Box D: The Development of International Crypto-Asset Capital and Liquidity Standards for Banks

The Basel Committee on Bank Supervision (BCBS) has proposed an approach to the prudential treatment of bank crypto-asset exposures.[174] This approach would include a system to classify crypto-assets into groups, with capital and liquidity requirements for each group that reflect their respective risks.[175] The proposed approach is informed by three principles: same risk, same activity, same treatment; simplicity; and minimum standards that allow jurisdictions to impose more stringent requirements and be considered compliant with the BCBS standard.

The proposed approach would generally apply different standards to crypto-assets under the different classifications. Under the proposed classification system, Group 1a would include tokenized traditional assets, such as an equity share that can be transferred via a blockchain, but that conveys the same legal rights as traditional ownership.[176] Group 1b would include crypto-assets with effective price stabilization mechanisms, such as some stablecoins.[177] Failure to meet Group 1a or Group 1b classification conditions on an ongoing basis would result in a crypto-asset being classified in Group 2.

Group 1a-specific classification conditions would include that the crypto-asset:

- is a digital representation of traditional assets that uses cryptography, distributed ledger technology, or similar technology to record ownership; and
- poses no more credit or market risk than the traditional asset, including by providing the same legal rights as direct ownership with no need to first redeem or convert the crypto-asset.

---

174 BCBS, *Second consultation on the prudential treatment of cryptoasset exposures,* June 2022, at https://www.bis.org/bcbs/publ/d533.pdf.

175 Please consult the full proposed standards for more detail.

176 Tokenized assets refer to crypto-assets that are digital representations of traditional assets using cryptography, DLT, or similar technology. They do not include ownership records maintained by a central depository or custodian.

177 BCBS would consider bank-issued tokenized payment assets that are backed by a bank's general assets rather than a specific reserve to be Group 1a crypto-assets.

Group 1b-specific classification conditions would include that the crypto-asset:

- is designed to be redeemable for a "peg value";[178]
- relies on a stabilization mechanism designed to minimize fluctuations in the crypto-asset's market value relative to the peg value and enable similar risk management as for traditional assets;
- includes sufficient information to verify ownership of the reserve assets;
- passes the redemption risk test (sufficient reserve assets to allow redemption for the peg value at all times) and the basis risk test (the crypto-asset holder can sell it for close to the peg value);
- is issued by an entity that is supervised and regulated by a supervisor that applies prudential capital and liquidity requirements (BCBS is considering this requirement as an alternative to the basis risk and redemption risk tests); and
- does not reference other crypto-assets or rely on protocols to change the crypto-asset's supply.[179]

Group 2a would include crypto-assets that meet the hedging recognition criteria of:

- being referenced by a regulated crypto-asset product,
- being highly liquid, and
- having sufficient price, trading volume, and market capitalization data over the previous year.

All other crypto-assets would be classified as Group 2b.

Crypto-assets that fail to meet the classification conditions would be subject to more stringent prudential standards. Group 2b crypto-assets, which also fail to meet the hedging recognition criteria, would be subject to particularly stringent standards, given the very high risks likely associated with such assets. If Group 2 exposures exceed 1 percent of Tier 1 Capital, all Group 2 exposures would be treated as Group 2b. Group 1a assets would be eligible for inclusion as high-quality liquid assets (HQLA) if the underlying, untokenized asset and the tokenized asset meet HQLA requirements whereas Group 1b, Group 2a, and Group 2b assets would not be eligible for inclusion as HQLA.

The BCBS published a first consultative document in June 2021 to seek stakeholder feedback on a preliminary proposal.[180] It issued a second consultative document in June 2022, which includes draft standards text.[181] Comments on the second consultative document were due by September 30, 2022, and the BCBS plans to finalize crypto-asset standards by the end of 2022. Given the rapid evolution and volatile nature of the crypto-asset market, the BCBS noted that it will continue to closely monitor developments during the consultation period. The standards that the BCBS aims to finalize around year-end

---

178 The peg value refers to a predefined amount of a reference asset or cash equal to the current market value of the reference asset.

179 Algorithmic stablecoins would fail the Group 1b classification condition.

180 BCBS, *Prudential treatment of cryptoasset exposures,* June 2021, at https://www.bis.org/bcbs/publ/d519.pdf.

181 BCBS, *Second consultation on the prudential treatment of cryptoasset exposures,* June 2022, at https://www.bis.org/bcbs/publ/d533.pdf.

2022 may be tightened if shortcomings in the consultation proposals are identified or new elements of risks emerge and based on the BCBS' overall assessment of the risks. Consequently, the final framework may differ from the framework proposed in June 2022.

BCBS standards are not automatically effective in the United States. Instead, the standards could become effective domestically by federal statute, or U.S. regulators would need to implement the standards through the notice and comment process in order for them to apply to U.S. banking organizations. The FDIC, FRB, and OCC will retain discretion to modify the standards to address the specific risks facing U.S. banking organizations and the U.S. financial system.

Trust Companies and National Trust Banks

Some crypto-asset firms have obtained charters as state trust companies or national trust banks. Such trust entities are limited in their interactions with crypto-asset activities insofar as they can only engage in activities that are authorized by state or federal law, consistent with applicable prudential requirements, and conducted in a safe and sound manner, as applicable. However, trust entities may be prohibited from making, or may choose not to make, commercial loans or accept deposits and may engage primarily in trust activities. Trust entities and their affiliates may not be subject to consolidated supervision or, in the case of state trust companies, federal regulation.[182]

Credit Unions

Like banks, credit unions are subject to restrictions on their activities and prudential requirements, which may limit the vulnerabilities that might arise from their interconnections with the crypto-asset ecosystem. For example, credit unions may only engage in the activities for which authority is granted to them by law, as determined by federal or state law and regulators. In addition to complying with specific prudential requirements, the NCUA is responsible for ensuring that federally insured credit unions operate in a safe and sound manner.

Regulatory Communications about the Scope of Permissible Activities and Prudential Requirements

As crypto-asset activities have expanded inside and outside the banking system, the FDIC, FRB, OCC, NCUA, and state banking regulators have taken steps to evaluate the risks involved to the safety and soundness of banks, while assessing the application of existing laws to crypto-assets. These regulators have issued several communications to banks, trust entities, and credit unions about these matters,

---

182 In certain circumstances, a trust entity that is engaged primarily in trust activities is not a "bank" under the Bank Holding Company Act and therefore its parent company, if there is one, is not a bank holding company. *See* 12 U.S.C. § 1841(c)(2)(D).

including, for example, the scope of permissible activities related to crypto-assets and associated prudential requirements.

The FDIC, FRB, and OCC have announced that they had engaged in interagency research and analysis to develop their "knowledge and understanding related to banking organizations' potential involvement in crypto-asset-related activities."[183]

The OCC has issued four interpretive letters on crypto-asset activities of national banks and federal savings associations.[184] The letters interpret existing law and communicate certain supervisory expectations. The letters confirm that, provided that national banks and federal savings associations comply with applicable law and conduct the activities in a safe and sound manner, those institutions may:

- provide "cryptocurrency" custody services, including facilitation of customers' "cryptocurrency" and "fiat" currency exchange transactions, transaction settlement, trade execution, record keeping, valuation, tax services, reporting, and other appropriate services;
- hold deposits that serve as reserves for stablecoins in certain circumstances;
- validate, store, and record payments transactions by serving as a node on independent node verification networks (INVNs), including distributed ledgers;
- use INVNs and related stablecoins to carry out permissible payments activities, including by buying, selling, and issuing stablecoins.

As noted in each letter, banks must comply with all applicable laws and regulations, such as AML/CFT requirements, fiduciary regulations, consumer protections and disclosures,[185] and, as with any other activity, operate in a safe and sound manner, including with respect to third-party risk management, liquidity risk, and operational risk.

---

183 FRB, FDIC, and OCC, "Joint Statement on Crypto-Asset Policy Sprint Initiative and Next Steps," November 23, 2021, at https://www.occ.gov/news-issuances/news-releases/2021/nr-ia-2021-120a.pdf.

184 OCC Interpretive Letter No. 1170, July 22, 2020, at https://www.occ.gov/topics/charters-and-licensing/interpretations-and-actions/2020/int1170.pdf. OCC Interpretive Letter No. 1172, September 21, 2020, at https://www.occ.gov/topics/charters-and-licensing/interpretations-and-actions/2020/int1172.pdf. OCC Interpretive Letter No. 1174, January 4, 2021, at https://www.occ.gov/news-issuances/news-releases/2021/nr-occ-2021-2a.pdf. OCC Interpretive Letter No. 1179, November 18, 2021, at https://www.occ.gov/topics/charters-and-licensing/interpretations-and-actions/2021/int1179.pdf (detailing a supervisory non-objection process that national banks and federal savings associations that plan to engage in the activities addressed by Interpretive Letters 1170, 1172, and 1174 should follow before commencing the activities).

185 With respect to stablecoin reserves held in deposit accounts, the OCC discussed disclosures regarding whether the deposits meet the requirements for pass-through insurance and are considered deposits of the individual stablecoin holder or deposits of the stablecoin issuer. For the requirements for deposit insurance to "pass through" to the individual stablecoin holders, see 12 C.F.R. Part 330 and FDIC General Counsel's Op. No. 8 (November 13, 2008), at https://www.fdic.gov/news/financial-institution-letters/2008/fil08129.html.

In its most recent Interpretive Letter on crypto-assets, the OCC informed national banks and federal savings associations that they should provide written notification to their supervisory office and receive written notification of no supervisory objection before engaging in the activities discussed in the prior Interpretive Letters.

The FDIC issued a Financial Institution Letter (FIL)[186] on crypto-related activities in April 2022 that communicated to FDIC-supervised institutions engaged in such activities that they should notify the FDIC with detailed information on the activity. The FIL noted that the FDIC will request information necessary to assess safety and soundness, financial stability, and consumer protection risks. It also communicated that FDIC-supervised institutions should be able to demonstrate that they can engage in crypto-asset-related activities in a safe and sound manner and encouraged FDIC-supervised institutions to notify their state regulators that they are engaged in these activities.

The FRB also issued a supervisory letter in August 2022 outlining the steps FRB-supervised banking organizations should take before engaging in crypto-asset-related activities, such as assessing whether such activities are legally permissible and determining whether any regulatory filings are required. Additionally, the supervisory letter states that FRB-supervised banking organizations should notify the FRB before engaging in crypto-asset-related activities. The supervisory letter also emphasizes that FRB-supervised banking organizations should have adequate systems and controls in place to conduct crypto-asset-related activities in a safe and sound manner prior to commencing such activities.[187]

The NCUA has issued two Letters to Credit Unions (LTCUs) on topics related to crypto-asset activities and DLT. The December 2021 LTCU provides clarity about the authority of federally insured credit unions (FICUs) to establish relationships with third-party providers that offer digital asset services to the FICUs' members, provided certain conditions are met, including compliance with all applicable laws.[188] The LTCU communicated the importance of credit unions exercising sound judgment and conducting necessary due diligence, risk assessment, and planning when choosing to introduce or bring together an outside vendor with its member. The May 2022 LTCU provides guidance clarifying expectations about credit unions'

186 FDIC, FIL-16-2022, "Notification of Engaging in Crypto-Related Activities," April 7, 2022, at https://www.fdic.gov/news/financial-institution-letters/2022/fil22016.html.

187 FRB, SR 22-6 / CA 22-6, "Engagement in Crypto-Asset-Related Activities by Federal Reserve-Supervised Banking Organizations," August 16, 2022, at https://www.federalreserve.gov/supervisionreg/srletters/SR2206.htm.

188 NCUA, 21-CU-16, "Relationships with Third Parties that Provide Services Related to Digital Assets," December 2021, at https://www.ncua.gov/regulation-supervision/letters-credit-unions-other-guidance/relationships-third-parties-provide-services-related-digital-assets.

use of DLT.[189] It also noted that use of DLT as an underlying technology by credit unions is not prohibited if it is deployed for permissible activities and in compliance with all applicable laws and regulations.

State bank regulators have issued determinations, regulations, or guidance indicating that state-chartered banks may engage in certain crypto-asset activities.[190] State regulators have emphasized the importance of continuous compliance with applicable law and safe and sound operation.

Charters and Licenses

At the state level, some states offer crypto-asset-specific bank and trust company charters. Wyoming has chartered four Special Purpose Depository Institutions (SPDIs) since 2019 and expects that "SPDIs will likely focus on digital assets, such as virtual currencies, digital securities and digital consumer assets."[191] Nebraska has also authorized the chartering of "digital asset depository institutions" and the operation of "digital asset depository departments" by certain traditional financial institutions. These entities may not be required to obtain deposit insurance and therefore they may not be regulated at the federal level.

In New York, entities chartered under the New York Banking Law may engage in "virtual currency" business activities only with the approval of the Superintendent of

---

189 NCUA, 22-CU-07, "Federally Insured Credit Union Use of Distributed Ledger Technologies," May 2022, at https://www.ncua.gov/regulation-supervision/letters-credit-unions-other-guidance/ federally-insured-credit-union-use-distributed-ledger-technologies.

190 *See, e.g.,* State of Washington Department of Financial Institutions, Division of Banks, "Statement from the Washington State Department of Financial Institutions, Division of Banks – Banking and Custody Services for Digital Assets," May 13, 2021, at https://dfi.wa.gov/sites/default/files/dob-statement-digital-assets.pdf. Texas Department of Banking, Industry Notice 2021-03, "Authority of Texas State-Chartered Banks to Provide Virtual Currency Custody Services to Customers," June 10, 2021, at https://www.dob.texas.gov/sites/default/files/files/news/Industrynotices/in2021-03.pdf. North Dakota Department of Financial Institutions, "Guidance for Digital Assets/Virtual Currency," May 18, 2022, at https://www.nd.gov/dfi/sites/www/files/documents/Regulatory%20Guidance/ Digital%20Asset%20Guidance%205-18-2022.pdf.

191 Wyoming Division of Banking, "Special Purpose Depository Institutions," at https:// wyomingbankingdivision.wyo.gov/banks-and-trust-companies/special-purpose-depository-institutions.

New York Department of Financial Services (NYDFS).[192] Pursuant to this authority, as of July 31, 2022, nine New York limited purpose trust companies (a charter type that pre-dates crypto-assets)[193] have received approval to engage in "virtual currency" business activities since 2015.[194] Because none of these entities have federal deposit insurance, they are not supervised at the federal level by the FDIC, and, if not part of depository institution holding companies, they are not subject to consolidated holding company supervision by the FRB.

A number of crypto-asset-focused firms have sought to obtain bank charters, and some crypto-asset-focused banks have sought to convert from state to federal charters. At the federal level, the OCC has granted conditional approvals for two conversions from state trust companies to uninsured national trust bank charters[195] and one preliminary conditional approval for a new uninsured national trust bank charter[196] to applicants engaged in or proposing to engage in significant crypto-asset activities. If not part of depository institution holding companies, these entities are not subject to consolidated holding company supervision by the FRB.

Third-Party Service Providers

Overall, bank regulators have tools to limit vulnerabilities arising from exposures to crypto-asset activities that might occur through banks' third-party service providers. The FDIC, FRB, OCC and most state bank regulators generally have regulatory and examination authority over certain services provided to banks to the same extent as if the bank conducted the activity itself, thereby providing visibility into

---

192 New York's BitLicense regulation limits virtual currency business activity to licensees but includes an exemption for "[p]ersons that are chartered under the New York Banking Law *and are approved by the superintendent to engage in Virtual Currency Business Activity.* N.Y. Comp. Codes R. & Regs. tit. 23, § 200.3 (emphasis added). "Virtual currency business activity" is defined as "any one of the following types of activities involving New York or a New York Resident: (1) receiving Virtual Currency for Transmission or Transmitting Virtual Currency, except where the transaction is undertaken for non-financial purposes and does not involve the transfer of more than a nominal amount of Virtual Currency; (2) storing, holding, or maintaining custody or control of Virtual Currency on behalf of others; (3) buying and selling Virtual Currency as a customer business; (4) performing Exchange Services as a customer business; or (5) controlling, administering, or issuing a Virtual Currency. The development and dissemination of software in and of itself does not constitute Virtual Currency Business Activity." N.Y. Comp. Codes R. & Regs. tit. 23, § 200.2(q).

193 NYDFS, "Organization of a Trust Company for the Limited Purpose of Exercising Fiduciary Powers," at https://www.dfs.ny.gov/apps_and_licensing/banks_and_trusts/procedure_certificate_merit_trust_comp.

194 NYDFS, "Virtual Currency Business," at https://www.dfs.ny.gov/virtual_currency_businesses.

195 OCC Conditional Approval #1257, January 13, 2021, at https://www.occ.gov/topics/charters-and-licensing/interpretations-and-actions/2021/ca1257.pdf. OCC Conditional Approval #1259, February 4, 2021, at https://www.occ.gov/topics/charters-and-licensing/interpretations-and-actions/2021/ca1259.pdf.

196 OCC Conditional Approval #1266, April 23, 2021, at https://www.occ.gov/topics/charters-and-licensing/interpretations-and-actions/2021/ca1266.pdf.

the risks arising from interconnections through service providers. The FDIC, FRB, and OCC have each provided guidance on relationships with third parties that communicates supervisory expectations regarding managing risks arising from these relationships.[197] These expectations apply to banks' current or potential third-party relationships, including for crypto-asset services.

The NCUA has limited authority to regulate or supervise third-party service providers used by credit unions, including credit union focused third-party service providers known as credit union service organizations (CUSOs). As a result, interconnections with crypto-asset activities may be able to grow more easily through CUSOs, relative to banks. The NCUA does not have enforcement authority over third-party service providers, including CUSOs, for cybersecurity, compliance with federal consumer financial protection laws and regulations, AML/CFT obligations, or prudential standards. As noted in part 5.3.2, Regulatory Arbitrage, the Council has previously recommended that Congress address this gap by providing NCUA with third-party vendor authority.[198]

4.2.3 Regulation of Other Selected Financial Institutions' Interactions with Crypto-Assets

Insurance Companies

Insurance regulators have taken some steps to limit vulnerabilities posed by insurers' interactions with crypto-assets. Regulation of the business of insurance in the United States is primarily conducted at the state level, [199] with some concurrent

---

197 *See, e.g.,* FDIC, "Outsourcing and Third-Party Providers (Vendor Management)," at https://www.fdic.gov/regulations/resources/director/risk/it-tpp.html. FRB, SR 13-19 / CA 13-21, "Guidance on Managing Outsourcing Risk," February 26, 2021, at https://www.federalreserve.gov/supervisionreg/srletters/sr1319.htm. OCC Bulletin 2013-29, "Third-Party Relationships: Risk Management Guidance," October 30, 2013, at https://www.occ.gov/news-issuances/bulletins/2013/bulletin-2013-29.html.

198 As discussed in the FSOC's 2021 Annual Report, the FHFA also has limited authority to regulate or supervise third-party service providers. Part 5.3.2, Regulatory Arbitrage, reiterates the FSOC's recommendation that Congress provide the FHFA with examination and enforcement authority for third-party service providers.

199 *See generally* the McCarran-Ferguson Act of 1945, 15 U.S.C. § 1011 *et seq.* State regulation of the insurance industry is coordinated through the National Association of Insurance Commissioners (NAIC), a voluntary organization with membership consisting of the chief insurance regulatory officials of the 50 states, the District of Columbia, and the five U.S. territories. Through the NAIC, the states develop model laws and implement an "accreditation program" to monitor adoption of those model laws deemed necessary by the states to "assure that an accredited state has sufficient authority to regulate the solvency of its multi-state domestic insurance industry in an effective manner." NAIC, "Financial Regulation Standards and Accreditation Program," April 2022, p. 7, at https://content.naic.org/sites/default/files/inline-files/FRSA%20Pamphlet%204-2022.pdf.

federal jurisdiction[200] and broad federal monitoring authority.[201] State laws and regulations limit the permissible investments available to insurance companies to ensure that insurers are able to satisfy payment obligations under their policies.[202] Certain crypto-asset investments are permissible, but survey data suggests that the extent of such investments remains relatively limited.[203] Moreover, insurers are barred under state law from including directly held "cryptocurrencies" as "admitted assets" that can contribute to available regulatory capital.[204]

Funds, Commodity Pools, and Advisers

Private funds, such as hedge funds, venture capital funds, and other types of investment vehicles like commodity pools,[205] are generally not specifically restricted by law or regulation from acquiring, investing in, or otherwise forming interconnections with crypto-assets. As a result, some of these investment vehicles are exposed to risks from extensive interconnections they have developed with crypto-asset activities.

Regulation limits the range of investors directly exposed to crypto-asset activities through private funds. Private funds have a small number of beneficial owners or are restricted to investors that are qualified purchasers; they may not offer securities to the general public. At the same time, the risks posed by private funds' interconnections with crypto-assets are difficult to ascertain because of limited

---

200 For example, variable annuities and variable life insurance products generally must be registered with the SEC (or qualify for an exemption from registration) before they are marketed, offered, or sold by insurers to investors.

201 Title V of the Dodd-Frank Act (the Federal Insurance Office Act) established the Federal Insurance Office (FIO) within Treasury. 31 U.S.C. § 313(a) *et seq.* The Director of FIO serves as a non-voting member of the FSOC and, among other authorities, the office is authorized to "monitor all aspects of the insurance industry, including identifying issues or gaps in the regulation of insurers that could contribute to a systemic crisis in the insurance industry or the U.S. financial system." 31 U.S.C. § 313(c)(1). The FIO Act also designates the Secretary of the Treasury as advisor to the President on "major domestic and international prudential policy issues in connection with all lines of insurance except health insurance." 31 U.S.C. § 321(a)(9).

202 *See, e.g.,* NAIC Investments of Insurers Model Act, at https://content.naic.org/sites/default/files/MO280.pdf.

203 Goldman Sachs, "Insurance Survey 2022," at https://www.gsam.com/content/gsam/us/en/institutions/market-insights/gsam-insights/2022/Insurance_Survey_2022.html.

204 *See* INT 21-01: "Accounting for Cryptocurrencies," Interpretation of the NAIC Statutory Accounting Principles Working Group (May 2021), at https://content.naic.org/sites/default/files/inline-files/INT%2021-01_2021-05.pdf, stating: "[D]irectly held cryptocurrencies do not meet the definition of an admitted asset and are therefore considered to be a nonadmitted asset for statutory accounting." The NAIC Accounting Practices and Procedures Manual, to which INT 21-01 applies, is incorporated by reference into the laws of all NAIC accredited jurisdictions.

205 The Commodity Exchange Act (CEA) defines a commodity pool as, "any investment trust, syndicate, or similar form of enterprise operated for the purpose of trading in commodity interests." 7 U.S.C. § 1a(10).

reporting and disclosure requirements. Private funds are exempt from investment company registration requirements that are designed to protect other types of investors. However, private fund advisers must typically register with the SEC or the appropriate state securities regulator unless they qualify for an exemption. In addition, advisers to private funds may be required to report certain information on Form PF, and proposed amendments, if adopted as proposed, would require advisers to report "digital assets" separately from other types of assets.[206]

Regulation also limits the range of investors directly exposed to crypto-asset activities through family offices. Family offices are companies that serve only family clients, are wholly owned by family clients, are exclusively controlled by one or more family members and/or family entities, and do not hold themselves out to the public as investment advisers. Typically, family offices are established by wealthy, financially sophisticated investors who are presumed to have sufficient financial experience and sophistication to act without the protection of the Investment Advisers Act of 1940. Family offices do not need to register as investment advisers, allowing greater flexibility in investment choices but limiting disclosure.

Finally, the CFTC's regulations similarly do not restrict or prohibit investment in crypto-asset derivatives by commodity pools.

The activities of family offices, funds, and commodity pools may indirectly be affected by the regulation and supervision of other financial institutions with which they interact. For example, if a hedge fund were to seek credit from a bank, regulation and supervision of that bank may indirectly influence the activities of the hedge fund. Specifically, the bank may reduce credit available to the fund or may impose some restrictions on the fund's use of loan proceeds if it perceives that the hedge fund is undertaking risky activity, pursuant to the interagency safety and soundness standards. However, banks and other traditional financial institutions may be unaware of the extent of their counterparties' crypto-asset exposures and risks.

4.2.4 Regulations Relating to Financial Products

Regulations governing the issuance or trading of financial products have significantly limited the vulnerabilities posed by interconnections between crypto-assets and the traditional financial system.

Securities Markets

The SEC and state securities regulators have jurisdiction over securities and securities-related conduct. The determination of whether a crypto-asset is a security

---

206 Form PF. Reporting Requirements for All Filers and Large Hedge Fund Advisers, 87 Fed. Reg. 53,832, September 1, 2022, at https://www.federalregister.gov/documents/2022/09/01/2022-17724/form-pf-reporting-requirements-for-all-filers-and-large-hedge-fund-advisers.

has important implications for the interactions of that crypto-asset with traditional financial markets. Persons engaged in certain activities involving crypto-assets that are securities have registration or other statutory or regulatory obligations under federal and state securities laws. The failure of market participants to comply with securities laws, whether relating to the offer and sale of crypto-assets that are securities or compliance with registration requirements applicable to exchanges, broker-dealers, and other intermediaries, means that banks and investors (including institutional investors) may face additional risk from engaging with these crypto-assets or intermediaries and exchanges that are engaging in activities in violation of the securities laws.

To the extent that interconnections develop between regulated securities markets and crypto-asset activities, compliance with securities laws would limit the risk of those interconnections. Unregistered securities may result in serious consumer and investor protection issues, including those described in Box E.

A wide range of instruments are securities under federal and state securities laws, including investment contracts and certain notes. Case law established various tests, such as the Howey test and the Reves test, which are used to determine whether instruments are considered securities under federal and state securities laws.[207]

Federal and state securities laws apply to crypto-assets that are securities. In 2017, the SEC stressed that the "U.S. federal securities law may apply to various activities, including distributed ledger technology, depending on the particular facts and circumstances, without regard to the form of the organization or technology used to effectuate a particular offer or sale."[208] This application extends to decentralized organizations.[209]

If a crypto-asset is a security, registration requirements generally apply to any primary offer or sale of that security by the issuer, an underwriter or other participant in the offering, and to any subsequent resale of such securities, including transactions on crypto-asset trading platforms. Exemptions from the registration requirements under federal and state securities laws may be available for primary offerings of securities and for resales of such securities if the conditions of those exemptions are met.[210] Offerings of securities made on a registered basis under the Securities Act of 1933 (Securities Act) require filing a registration statement with the SEC. A registration statement's prospectus must disclose the transaction's material terms and the issuer's business, including financial statements. When offerings

---

207 *SEC v. W.J. Howey Co.*, 328 U.S. 293, 301 (1946). Reves v. Ernst & Young, 494 U.S. 56 (1990).

208 SEC, *Report of Investigation Pursuant to Section 21(a) of the Securities Exchange Act of 1934: The DAO*, Exchange Act Release No. 81207, July 25, 2017, p. 10, at https://www.sec.gov/litigation/investreport/34-81207.pdf.

209 *Id.*, p. 18, at https://www.sec.gov/litigation/investreport/34-81207.pdf.

210 Banks are exempt from the registration requirements of the Securities Act but not the anti-fraud and anti-manipulation provisions.

rely on exemptions from the registration requirements of the Securities Act, the disclosures available to investors vary depending on the specific exemption being relied upon.

The issuer of a security, including a crypto-asset that is a security, may also become subject to the periodic and current reporting requirements of the Securities Exchange Act of 1934 (Exchange Act). These reporting requirements may arise either because, depending on the characteristics of a security or where it is traded, among other factors, the issuer of a security (i) is required to register the crypto-asset as a class of security under the Exchange Act or (ii) has registered an offering of the crypto-asset under the Securities Act. In these cases, an entity must file certain reports with the SEC, including annual, periodic, and current reports. These reports are available to the public through the SEC's EDGAR database. These entities may also be subject to other Exchange Act disclosure requirements, such as those relating to proxy solicitations and tender offers.

Finally, for a crypto-asset security to trade on an exchange, the exchange must be registered, and the issuer must meet the exchange's listing standards.[211] The SEC must approve these listing standards and trading rules as being consistent with the Exchange Act. These requirements may limit the extent and risks of interconnections between crypto-assets and the traditional financial system by limiting the availability of crypto-asset exposures that do not meet requirements under securities laws. For example, to date, the SEC has not approved a proposal by a national securities exchange to list and trade a spot Bitcoin ETF.

Securities exchanges are discussed further in part 4.4, Regulations Relating to Financial Exposures via Interconnections within the Crypto-Asset Ecosystem.

Commodities Markets

The Commodity Exchange Act (CEA) establishes a federal regulatory regime overseen by the CFTC for derivatives transactions. Regulations imposed under the CEA limit risks posed by interconnections between crypto-asset activities and derivatives markets. However, a regulatory gap exists in spot markets for crypto-assets that are commodities and not securities, as detailed in part 5.3.1, Regulation of the Spot Market for Crypto-Assets that are not Securities.

---

211 *See* SEC, *Report of Investigation Pursuant to Section 21(a) of the Securities Exchange Act of 1934: The DAO*, Exchange Act Release No. 81207 (July 25, 2017). *In re Zachary Coburn: Order Instituting Cease-and-Desist Proceedings Pursuant to Section 21C of the Securities Exchange Act of 1934, Making Findings, and Imposing a Cease-and-Desist Order*, Exchange Act Release No. 84553 (November 8, 2018). *SEC v. Bitqyck, Inc., et al.* (complaint filed on August 29, 2019, in U.S. District Court, Northern District of Texas, Dallas Division). *In re Poloniex LLC: Order Instituting Cease-and-Desist Proceedings Pursuant to Section 21C of the Securities Exchange Act of 1934, Making Findings, and Imposing a Cease-and-Desist Order*, Exchange Act Release No. 92607 (August 9, 2021).

The CEA defines "commodity" broadly. It does not limit the term to tangible or physical commodities but rather defines it to include generally all "goods and articles ... and all services, rights, and interests ... in which contracts for future delivery are presently or in the future dealt in."[212] In 2014, the CFTC Chairman first signaled that certain crypto-assets, namely "virtual currencies," are commodities as defined under the CEA.[213] In 2015, the CFTC formally took the position that "Bitcoin and other virtual currencies are encompassed in the [CEA] definition and properly defined as commodities."[214] Since then, multiple judicial decisions have affirmed that "virtual currencies" such as a Bitcoin meet the definition of a commodity under the CEA.[215]

The CEA grants the CFTC exclusive jurisdiction over most transactions involving commodity derivatives. A commodity derivative is a financial instrument, such as a futures contract or swap, whose value is based on the price of an underlying commodity. Most derivatives are required to be traded on a Designated Contract Market (DCM) or Swap Execution Facility (SEF) registered with the CFTC, and the trades must be cleared through a Derivatives Clearing Organization (DCO) also registered with the CFTC. These requirements apply equally to crypto-asset derivatives, which do not receive different treatment under CFTC laws and regulations.

Importantly, the CFTC's jurisdiction over the spot market for commodities is more limited, as is discussed in detail in part 5.3.1, Regulation of the Spot Market for Crypto-Assets that are not Securities, but it maintains general anti-fraud and manipulation enforcement authority over the spot market, as well as jurisdiction over certain types of spot transactions that are legally treated as if they were futures transactions. Specifically, absent an exception, certain spot transactions known as "retail commodity transactions" conducted on a leveraged or margined basis are

---

212 7 U.S.C. § 1a(9). Many securities also fall within the definition of commodity set out by the CEA. However, the CEA and the Dodd-Frank Act contain provisions that preserve the SEC's jurisdiction and confirm that securities laws continue to apply to securities and security-based swaps.

213 *See* Chairman Timothy Massad, Testimony Before the U.S. Senate Committee on Agriculture, Nutrition & Forestry, December 10, 2014, at https://www.cftc.gov/PressRoom/SpeechesTestimony/opamassad-6.

214 In the Matter of: Coinflip, Inc., d/b/a Derivabit, and Francisco Riordan, CFTC Docket No. 15-29, September 17, 2015, at https://www.cftc.gov/sites/default/files/idc/groups/public/@lrenforcementactions/documents/legalpleading/enfcoinfliprorder09172015.pdf.

215 *See, e.g. CFTC v. McDonnell*, 287 F. Supp. 3d 213, 217 (E.D.N.Y. 2018) ("Virtual currencies can be regulated by CFTC as a commodity.... They fall well-within the common definition of 'commodity' as well as the [CEA's] definition of 'commodities' as 'all other goods and articles ... in which contracts for future delivery are presently or in the future dealt in.'"). *McDonnell*, 332 F. Supp. 3d at 650–51 (entering judgment against Proposed Defendant following bench trial). *CFTC v. My Big Coin Pay, Inc.,* 334 F. Supp. 3d 492, 495–98 (D. Mass. 2018) (denying motion to dismiss. determining that a non-bitcoin virtual currency is a "commodity" under the CEA).

treated as futures transactions and must occur on a CFTC-regulated exchange,[216] which helps to ensure adequate investor protection. One exception applies to futures contracts that result in "actual delivery" of the commodity within 28 days or such other longer period as the CFTC may establish by rule or regulation.

In March 2020, the CFTC issued final interpretative guidance on the meaning of "actual delivery" in the context of crypto-assets.[217] Under that guidance, actual delivery occurs when a customer secures possession and control of the entire quantity of the commodity, the customer has the ability to use the entire quantity of the commodity freely in commerce, and the offeror and counterparty seller do not retain any interest in, legal right, or control over any of the commodity.[218]

Crypto-asset derivatives products in CFTC-regulated markets include contracts for Bitcoin and Ether futures products, initially introduced in 2017 through self-certification by the Chicago Mercantile Exchange Inc. (CME) and other DCMs. In 2018, the CFTC released a staff advisory that set out guidance for CFTC-registered entities seeking to list or clear "virtual currency" derivatives products.[219] The advisory aimed to encourage innovation and growth in "virtual currency" derivatives products but within an appropriate oversight framework. The advisory provided guidance to exchanges and clearinghouses on certain enhancements when listing a derivatives contract based on a "virtual currency." CFTC staff highlighted key areas that require particular attention in the context of listing a new virtual currency derivatives contract, including: (1) enhanced market surveillance; (2) coordination with CFTC staff; (3) large trader reporting; (4) outreach to stakeholders; and (5) DCO risk management.

Commodities futures laws and regulations limit the vulnerabilities presented by connections between institutions in the regulated derivatives market and the crypto-asset ecosystem by, for example, providing core principles for contract design and exchange and clearinghouse operation. Regulated institutions, such as DCOs, that comply with applicable laws and regulations and appropriately manage their risks, are unlikely to amplify shocks like a counterparty default. Similarly, financial resources requirements applicable to DCOs are also designed to help mitigate the risks that clearinghouses face.

The CFTC has brought more than 50 enforcement actions in the crypto-asset space since 2014, including anti-fraud actions discussed in Box E, Market Integrity

---

216 7 U.S.C. § 2(c)(2)(D). Generally, retail commodity transactions are commodity transactions entered into with or offered to persons other than eligible contract participants or eligible commercial entities on a leveraged, margined, or financed basis.

217 Retail Commodity Transactions Involving Certain Digital Assets, 85 Fed. Reg. 37,734 (June 24, 2020), at https://www.cftc.gov/sites/default/files/2020/06/2020-11827a.pdf.

218 Id.

219 CFTC Staff Advisory No. 18-14, "Advisory with respect to Virtual Currency Derivative Product Listings," May 21, 2018, at https://www.cftc.gov/node/214951.

and Consumer and Investor Protections.[220] For example, the CFTC has ordered exchanges to pay civil monetary penalties for offering illegal off-exchange financed retail commodity transactions in Bitcoin and other crypto-assets and for failing to register as futures commission merchants (FCMs).[221] The CFTC has also enforced laws prohibiting abusive trading practices such as wash trading and prearranged trades on a derivatives platform.[222]

4.3 Regulations Relating to Crypto-Asset Pricing Dynamics

Investors' risk appetite and the degree of speculative trading tend to be dominant factors in driving crypto-asset prices. The discussion of crypto-asset prices in part 3.3.1, Crypto-Asset Prices, emphasized these factors, especially considering a general lack of economic fundamentals to guide the prices of many crypto-assets. One of the primary goals of markets regulation is to support accurate price discovery.

Box E discusses significant concerns about market integrity and consumer and investor protection posed by crypto-assets, including pricing dynamics related to fraud or market manipulation. Indeed, the CFTC, SEC, CFPB, and FDIC have warned investors, market participants, and consumers about crypto-assets, including the potential for asset price volatility.[223] Among other subjects, these warnings have noted that volatility in asset prices can cause investors to lose money on crypto-asset investments, that crypto-asset prices can be affected by large trades placed by an individual or a coordinated group, and that investors may be drawn into the market based on "FOMO"—fear of missing out—during large price increases.

---

220 CFTC Chairman Rostin Benham, Keynote Address at the Brookings Institution Webcast on the Future of Crypto Regulation, July 25, 2022, at https://www.cftc.gov/PressRoom/SpeechesTestimony/opabehnam24.

221 CFTC, Release Number 8450-21, "CFTC Orders Tether and Bitfinex to Pay Fines Totaling $42.5 Million," October 15, 2021, at https://www.cftc.gov/PressRoom/PressReleases/8450-21. CFTC, Release Number 8433-21, "CFTC Imposes A $1.25 Million Penalty against Kraken for Offering Illegal Off-Exchange Digital Asset Trading and Failing to Register as Required," September 28, 2021, at https://www.cftc.gov/PressRoom/PressReleases/8433-21.

222 In the Matter of: TeraExchange LLC, CFTC Docket No. 15-33, September 24, 2015, at https://www.cftc.gov/sites/default/files/idc/groups/public/@lrenforcementactions/documents/legalpleading/enfteraexchangeorder92415.pdf.

223 CFTC, "A CFTC Primer on Virtual Currencies," October 17, 2017, at https://www.cftc.gov/sites/default/files/idc/groups/public/documents/file/labcftc_primercurrencies100417.pdf. SEC, "Digital Asset and "Crypto" Investment Scams – Investor Alert," September 1, 2021, at https://www.sec.gov/oiea/investor-alerts-and-bulletins/digital-asset-and-crypto-investment-scams-investor-alert. CFPB, "CFPB Warns Consumers about Bitcoin," August 11, 2014, at https://www.consumerfinance.gov/about-us/newsroom/cfpb-warns-consumers-about-bitcoin/. FDIC, "Advisory to FDIC-Insured Institutions Regarding FDIC Deposit Insurance and Dealings with Crypto Companies," July 29, 2022, at https://www.fdic.gov/news/financial-institution-letters/2022/fil22035b.pdf.

Additional regulations discussed in this report may also affect asset prices. Regulation related to leverage, discussed in part 4.7, Regulations Relating to Leverage, may limit the amount of leverage speculators can obtain, dampening their potential impact on price movements. For example, banks may limit extensions of credit to overheated asset markets pursuant to the interagency safety and soundness standards. More generally, regulation that reduces opacity in the crypto-asset ecosystem, such as SEC public reporting requirements and public monthly reserve asset attestations for NYDFS-approved stablecoin issuers, may provide information that affects how market participants price assets. Clarity about interconnections within the crypto-asset ecosystem (part 4.4, Regulations Relating to Financial Exposures via Interconnections within the Crypto-Asset Ecosystem) could cause investors to exercise additional caution and mitigate the risk of asset price bubbles. However, these benefits will only arise to the extent that market participants are subject to, and comply with, such requirements.

Finally, accounting standards may assist market participants in pricing assets by providing them with decision-useful and consistent information. Accounting standards under the U.S. generally accepted accounting principles (GAAP) and International Financial Reporting Standards (IFRS) are principles-based and apply across all transactions and arrangements. There is no crypto-asset specific approach. Under GAAP, crypto-assets generally meet the definition of indefinite-lived intangibles and, as a result, are not measured at fair value on a recurring basis. Instead, they are tested for impairment annually or more frequently if events or changes in circumstances indicate that it is more likely than not that the asset is impaired. Specific specialized industry accounting standards may apply to certain entities. For example, investment companies generally measure crypto-assets they hold as an investment at fair value. SEC Staff Accounting Bulletin 121 (SAB 121), discussed further in part 4.6, Regulations Relating to Funding Mismatches and Risk of Runs, provides interpretive guidance for SEC filers and certain other companies that safeguard crypto-assets for customers. As a result, there could be a diversity of accounting classification and reporting, which may have repercussions on the evaluation and representation of crypto-asset activities in financial statements. The Financial Accounting Standards Board (FASB) has added a standard-setting project to its technical agenda related to the accounting for and disclosure of crypto-assets.

Box E: Market Integrity and Consumer and Investor Protection

Crypto-asset markets present significant concerns related to market integrity and consumer and investor protection.[224] Lapses in market integrity or consumer and investor protection are conceptually distinct from financial stability vulnerabilities that amplify shocks and spread financial losses. However, elements of market integrity and consumer and investor protection may be related to financial stability. Consumers and investors may be

---

224 Consumer and investor protections are discussed in more detail by United States Department of the Treasury, *Crypto-Assets: Implications for Consumers, Investors, and Businesses*, September 2022, at https://home.treasury.gov/system/files/136/CryptoAsset_EO5.pdf.

affected by the amplification of shocks. For example, certain crypto-asset prices might fall in price in response to a shock such as the revelation of fraud related to that crypto-asset. Consumers and investors may also be negatively impacted if a shock leads to the freezing of withdrawals at a major platform, especially if that platform had misrepresented the safety of investments in it.

Financial regulators have noted several significant concerns with the crypto-asset ecosystem, including that unregistered crypto-asset platforms, because they are not complying with applicable laws and regulations, are not protecting market participants against abuse.[225] The incidence of fraud has also led to a Congressional investigation.[226]

Securities Markets

Certain crypto-assets are securities. Therefore, such crypto-assets are subject to U.S. federal and state securities laws and must meet securities law requirements or qualify for an exemption from such requirements, as described in part 4.2.4, Regulations Relating to Financial Products. Securities laws are designed to further market integrity and investor protection in several ways. Disclosure requirements are designed to ensure that investors have timely, accurate, and complete information about securities being offered. They also act as a check against conflicts of interest or self-dealing. Trading rules on securities exchanges limit abusive, fraudulent, or manipulative trading practices. Exchange rules, self-regulatory organization (SRO) rules, and securities laws play a key role in addressing conflicts of interest, the suitability of assets for investors, price discovery, fair and efficient trading, and the disclosure of trade information. Securities exchanges and their rules are subject to SEC oversight, including with respect to their governance, membership qualifications, trading rules, disciplinary procedures, recordkeeping, and fees. Clients of registered broker-dealers generally also benefit from protections in the event of the loss of cash or securities, subject to limits, through the Securities Investor Protection Corporation (SIPC).

The SEC and state securities regulators have taken a number of actions to protect consumers, investors, and markets. As of July 31, 2022, the SEC had brought a total of 96 crypto-asset-related enforcement actions.[227] State securities regulators have brought numerous enforcement actions as well, many of which have been coordinated through the North American Securities Administrators Association (NASAA), a nonprofit

---

225 CFTC, "A CFTC Primer on Virtual Currencies," October 17, 2017, at http://www.cftc.gov/idc/groups/public/documents/file/labcftc_primercurrencies100417.pdf. SEC, "Digital Asset and "Crypto" Investment Scams – Investor Alert" September 1, 2021, at https://www.sec.gov/oiea/investor-alerts-and-bulletins/digital-asset-and-crypto-investment-scams-investor-alert. CFPB, "CFPB Warns Consumers About Bitcoin," August 11, 2014, at https://www.consumerfinance.gov/about-us/newsroom/cfpb-warns-consumers-about-bitcoin/. FDIC, "FDIC Issues a Fact Sheet to the Public on FDIC Insurance and Crypto Companies", July 29, 2022, at https://www.fdic.gov/news/press-releases/2022/pr22058.html.

226 House Committee on Oversight and Reform, "Chairman Krishnamoorthi Requests Information from Federal Agencies and Crypto Exchanges on Efforts to Combat Fraud and Scams," August 30, 2022, at https://oversight.house.gov/news/press-releases/chairman-krishnamoorthi-requests-information-from-federal-agencies-and-crypto.

227 See SEC, Crypto Assets and Cyber Enforcement Actions, at https://www.sec.gov/spotlight/cybersecurity-enforcement-actions.

association of state and provincial securities regulators. In a recent three-year period, NASAA's U.S. member securities regulators initiated over 480 investigations and brought more than 145 enforcement actions involving crypto-assets (including actions against market makers, crypto-asset issuers, lending and selling platforms, mining pools, and solicitors/unregistered brokers). In addition, in April 2018, NASAA organized a task force of its member state and provincial securities regulators to begin a coordinated series of investigations of "cryptocurrency"-related products known as Operation Cryptosweep.[228]

These statistics indicate that non-compliance with securities laws has been widespread in the crypto-asset ecosystem. Many crypto-assets have been, or may currently be, offered and sold in unregistered offerings and on unregistered crypto-asset platforms without required disclosures or market oversight. Over the past several years, certain crypto-asset market participants have violated the registration provisions of federal and state securities laws by offering and selling crypto-assets that were securities in the United States without registration or reliance upon an available exemption. Lack of compliance poses risks to market integrity and leaves investors vulnerable by depriving them of important disclosures and other protections.

In addition, all securities offerings and transactions, whether registered or exempt, are subject to the anti-fraud provisions of the U.S. federal securities laws and to various anti-fraud provisions in state securities laws. Investors can bring actions under certain provisions of the U.S. federal securities laws, and remedies are available to investors if the offerings are not registered with the SEC under the Securities Act or made pursuant to an available exemption from such requirements. For example, if a purchaser were sold a security in violation of the registration provisions of the Securities Act, the purchaser may be entitled to damages. Moreover, the Securities Act prohibits touting a security in exchange for consideration without fully disclosing the receipt and amount of consideration.

Commodities and Derivatives Markets

The mission of the CFTC is to promote the integrity, resilience, and vibrancy of the U.S. commodity derivatives markets through sound regulation, including protecting investors and the public from fraud. The CEA includes a number of requirements related to market integrity and investor protection. For example, DCMs and SEFs may only permit trading in contracts and swaps that are not readily susceptible to manipulation. Trading rules on DCMs and SEFs seek to ensure market integrity by prohibiting manipulative and abusive trading behavior. Regulation of DCOs is intended to protect market participants against the credit risk of counterparties.

The CFTC has authority to investigate and bring enforcement actions for fraud and manipulation and for violations of CFTC regulations that provide consumer and market protections. The CFTC has used this authority on many occasions over the past several years in crypto-asset derivatives markets and in the spot market for crypto-assets that are not securities. For example, the CFTC ordered the largest stablecoin issuer at the time to pay a penalty for making untrue or misleading statements and omitting material facts in

---

228 *See* NASAA, "Operation Cryptosweep," at https://www.nasaa.org/policy/enforcement/operation-cryptosweep/.

connection with a stablecoin it issued.[229] Ultimately, the CFTC has brought over 50 crypto-asset-related enforcement actions and imposed millions of dollars in penalties in cases involving fraud, pump-and-dumps, and Ponzi schemes.[230]

Consumer Protection and Consumer Confusion

Several consumer protection laws may apply to crypto-asset products and services at the federal and state levels. For example, the Dodd-Frank Act prohibits unfair, deceptive, or abusive acts or practices (UDAAP) by persons offering or providing consumer financial products or services (covered persons) and persons that provide certain material services (service providers) to covered persons' offering or provisioning of consumer financial products or services.[231]

In particular, consumers may be unaware that crypto-assets are not insured, particularly when crypto-asset platforms refer to customer accounts as "deposits."[232] Federal deposit insurance is only available for bank deposits and certain credit union deposits, through the FDIC and the NCUA, respectively, and is only applicable in the event the bank or credit union fails. Deceptive advertising and misleading statements, such as misleading use of the FDIC's name or logo in promotional materials, can increase customer confusion.[233] The CFPB has clarified that misuse of the name or logo of the FDIC, engaging in false advertising, or making misrepresentations to consumers about deposit insurance likely violates the CFPB's prohibition on deception,[234] regardless of whether the conduct is engaged in knowingly.[235]

---

229 CFTC, Release Number 8450-21, "CFTC Orders Tether and Bitfinex to Pay Fines Totaling $42.5 Million," October 15, 2021, at https://www.cftc.gov/PressRoom/PressReleases/8450-21.

230 For example, on September 21, 2017, the CFTC filed a complaint in federal court in the Southern District of New York against Nicholas Gelfman and Gelfman Blueprint, Inc., which resulted in court orders for restitution and civil money penalties. Complaint for Injunctive and Other Equitable Relief and for Civil Monetary Penalties under the Commodity Exchange Act and Commission Regulations, *Commodity Futures Trading Comm'n v. Gelfman Blueprint, Inc., and Nicholas Gelfman*, No. 17-7181 (S.D.N.Y. Sept. 21, 2017), at https://www.cftc.gov/sites/default/files/idc/groups/public/@lrenforcementactions/documents/legalpleading/enfgelfmancomplaint09212017.pdf. *Commodity Futures Trading Comm'n v. Gelfman Blueprint, Inc.*, No. 17-7181, (S.D.N.Y. Oct. 16, 2018), at https://www.cftc.gov/sites/default/files/2018-10/enfgelfmanfinaljudgment101618.pdf. Consent Order for Permanent Injunction, Civil Monetary Penalty, and Other Equitable Relief, *Commodity Futures Trading Comm'n v. Gelfman Blueprint, Inc.*, No. 17-7181 (PKC), 2018 WL 6320653, (S.D.N.Y. Oct. 2, 2018), at https://www.cftc.gov/sites/default/files/2018-10/enfgelfmanblueprintconsentorder100218.pdf.

231 The definition of consumer financial product is broad, but it excludes advisory services related to securities provided by a person regulated by the SEC or a state securities commissioner.

232 Molly White, "Excerpts from Letters to the Judge in the Voyager Digital Bankruptcy Case," July 23, 2022, at https://blog.mollywhite.net/voyager-letters/.

233 *See* CFPB, Consumer Financial Protection Circular 2022-02, "Deceptive Representations Involving the FDIC's Name or Logo or Deposit Insurance," May 17, 2022, at https://www.consumerfinance.gov/compliance/circulars/circular-2022-02-deception-representations-involving-the-fdics-name-or-logo-or-deposit-insurance/.

234 *See id.*

235 Such misrepresentations also may violate the Federal Deposit Insurance Act and 12 C.F.R. Part 328.

In response to potential customer confusion, the FDIC has issued an advisory to FDIC-insured banks to, among other things, monitor and confirm that crypto-asset companies with which they have business dealings do not misrepresent the availability of deposit insurance and take appropriate action should such a misrepresentation occur.[236] The advisory noted that "[t]he FDIC is concerned about the risks of consumer confusion or harm arising from crypto assets offered by, through, or in connection with insured depository institutions [(IDIs)]. Risks are elevated when a non-bank entity offers crypto assets to the non-bank's customers while offering an [IDI's] deposit products. Inaccurate representations about deposit insurance by non-banks, including crypto-asset companies, may confuse the non-bank's customers and cause those customers to mistakenly believe they are protected against any type of loss. Moreover, non-bank customers may not understand the role of the bank as it relates to the activities of the non-bank, or the speculative nature of certain crypto assets as compared to deposit products."[237] The FDIC and the NCUA have also issued materials for the public on deposit insurance and crypto companies.[238] In addition, the FDIC has issued cease and desist letters, including one joint letter with the FRB, to crypto-asset platforms and websites for making false and misleading statements about FDIC deposit insurance.[239]

Finally, consumers may be unaware of redemption restrictions on stablecoins. U.S. retail customers cannot directly redeem the two largest stablecoins for dollars.[240] Stablecoin holders who lack redemption rights may be unable to find willing counterparties to exit their stablecoin positions.

---

236 FDIC, FIL-35-2022, "Advisory to FDIC-Insured Institutions Regarding Deposit Insurance and Dealings with Crypto Companies," July 29, 2022, at https://www.fdic.gov/news/financial-institution-letters/2022/fil22035.html.

237 FDIC, "Advisory to FDIC-Insured Institutions Regarding Deposit Insurance and Dealings with Crypto Companies," July 29, 2022, p. 1, at https://www.fdic.gov/news/financial-institution-letters/2022/fil22035b.pdf.

238 FDIC, PR-58-2022, "FDIC Issues a Fact Sheet to the Public on FDIC Deposit Insurance and Crypto Companies," July 29, 2022, at https://www.fdic.gov/news/press-releases/2022/pr22058.html. NCUA, "Cryptocurrency and Other Digital Assets," July 25, 2022, at https://www.mycreditunion.gov/financial-resources/cryptocurrency-digital-assets.

239 FDIC, PR-60-2022, "FDIC Issues Cease and Desist Letters to Five Companies For Making Crypto-Related False or Misleading Representations about Deposit Insurance," August 19, 2022, at https://www.fdic.gov/news/press-releases/2022/pr22060.html. FDIC and FRB, "Joint Letter Regarding Potential Violations of Section 18(a)(4) of the Federal Deposit Insurance Act," July 28, 2022, at https://www.federalreserve.gov/newsevents/pressreleases/files/bcreg20220728a1.pdf.

240 Tether states that it does not allow any U.S. user to redeem Tether. Circle does not allow U.S. retail users to redeem USD Coin, only institutional users. *See, e.g.,* Senate Banking, Housing and Urban Affairs Committee, Hearing on Stablecoins, CQ Congressional Transcripts, Dec. 14, 2021, comments by Chief Strategy Officer at Circle, Dante Disparte. ("Circle's counterparties, as a company, are other institutions and companies. We don't face the retail market as a retail payment system.") and Tether, "U.S. Residents,"at https://tether.to/en/us-residents/. ("Unfortunately, Tether has decided to stop serving U.S. individual and corporate customers altogether. As of January 1, 2018, no issuance or redeeming services will be available to these users. Exceptions to these provisions may be made by Tether, in its sole discretion, for entities that are: Established or organized outside of the United States or its territorial or insular possessions; and, Eligible Contract Participants pursuant to U.S. law.")

4.4 Regulations Relating to Financial Exposures via Interconnections within the Crypto-Asset Ecosystem

Large crypto-asset platforms pose significant financial stability risks inside the crypto-asset ecosystem through their numerous interconnections and risk management profiles, as discussed in part 3.3.2, Financial Exposures via Interconnections within the Crypto-Asset Ecosystem.

Most crypto-asset platforms are not currently registered under the securities laws or the CEA. Such registration would trigger regulatory obligations, including financial adequacy requirements, clearinghouse guaranty funds, recordkeeping, and regular reporting and supervision. These obligations would likely affect the risks posed by a platform to its counterparties.

A crypto-asset platform that meets the Exchange Act definition of "exchange" by matching orders in securities (including crypto-asset securities) of multiple buyers and sellers is required to register with the SEC as a national securities exchange or obtain an appropriate exemption. Registration as an exchange would require a platform to acquire self-regulatory capacity. In addition, depending on the facts and circumstances, a crypto-asset platform that combines additional functions might be required, depending on the nature of the activity, to register with the SEC in another capacity, potentially as an investment company, clearing agency, or broker-dealer. Registration as a broker-dealer would subject a crypto-asset intermediary to the rules of the Financial Industry Regulatory Authority (FINRA) (the SRO for the OTC markets) as well as any exchange on which the broker-dealer might participate. Regardless of any characterization or assertion of "decentralization," applicable regulatory frameworks still apply to participants and activities.[241]

Certain crypto-asset platforms are likely listing securities and are not in compliance with exchange, broker-dealer, or other registration requirements.[242] While each crypto-asset's legal status depends on its own facts and circumstances, it is unlikely that a platform trading a large number of crypto-assets is not trading any crypto-assets that are securities. Registration requirements apply based on the function performed, such as facilitating the trading of securities, without regard to the type of securities, the technology used, or whether a platform has the appearance of, or purports to be, decentralized. For the reasons discussed in part 4.2.4, Regulations Relating to Financial Products, the securities laws may reduce the extent and risks of interconnections between the crypto-asset ecosystem and the traditional financial system.

---

241 *In the Matter of Zachary Coburn,* Exchange Act Release No. 84553 (Nov. 8, 2018), at https://www.sec.gov/litigation/admin/2018/34-84553.pdf.

242 Exchanges that list traditional securities and crypto-asset securities are subject to the same laws. Compliance with requirements for registered exchanges may mitigate crypto-asset risks.

Registration and other requirements also apply to various entities in the commodities derivatives market, including trading organizations—DCMs and SEFs—and DCOs. Similar requirements apply to various intermediaries, such as FCMs and swap dealers. This framework may affect the risks of interconnections within the crypto-asset ecosystem by acting as a screen that limits both the impact of noncompliant activities and the risks posed by compliant actors. Such regulations include prohibitions on permitting trading in products that are readily susceptible to manipulation and minimum adjusted net capital requirements.

All futures contracts must be cleared through a registered DCO, which may limit the risks of interconnections within the crypto-asset ecosystem by reducing the likelihood that the shock of a single counterparty's default will be amplified. With respect to swaps, subject to CFTC review, DCOs are presumed eligible to accept swaps that are within a group, category, type, or class of swaps that the DCO already clears. For other swaps, DCOs must request approval from the CFTC, and the CFTC considers the DCO's financial resources and ability to manage risks associated with clearing the swap. This may limit the availability of crypto-asset swaps and reduce risk from interconnections.

Many large platforms that currently operate in the U.S. emphasize that they are regulated as money services businesses (MSBs). MSB regulation is not designed for the purpose of comprehensively mitigating vulnerabilities arising from the potential failure of a large, interconnected platform, or for other purposes, such as market integrity. Obligations at the federal level focus on anti-money laundering controls, and state-level obligations are intended to provide consumer protection related to money transmission. Though FinCEN's MSB regulations generally apply to money transmission denominated in crypto-assets, state money transmitter laws vary considerably, with some exempting crypto-assets entirely. In addition, whether specific financial activities fall under the jurisdiction of FinCEN or a state depends on facts and circumstances. Certain crypto-asset activities may not be subject to FinCEN's MSB regulations or state money transmission requirements, particularly those not involving the transfer of funds (e.g., a platform that matches buyers and sellers and where the parties settle the transaction through an outside venue), although they may fall under other regulatory regimes, such as those applicable to securities or commodities brokers.

State-level MSB laws might affect the capital positions of platforms that are MSBs through requirements to maintain a minimum net worth or surety bonds. However, these requirements typically form only very limited loss absorbing buffers for the purpose of consumer protection of money transmission activities, and states differ widely in the strength and application of these requirements. The Conference of State Bank Supervisors (CSBS) model Money Transmission Modernization Act (MTMA) includes prudential standards appropriate for large institutions, including a tangible shareholders equity requirement that scales with the size of the institution[243] and a requirement that companies hold an equivalent amount of customer funds in safe, permissible investments.[244] State regulators approved the MTMA in August 2021. To date, one state has adopted the MTMA, while other states are actively seeking to implement provisions of the model law via legislation or regulation. Most states currently have static net worth requirements, and most states require that customer funds be protected by permissible investments. In addition, unlike the FDIC's authorities for resolving banks or Securities Investor Protection Act (SIPA) liquidations for broker-dealers, MSB laws generally make no provision for the orderly resolution of large, interconnected entities in any manner except through bankruptcy.

State-level MSB laws may not otherwise limit the licensed entity's activities outside of money transmission, unlike, for example, bank charters. MSB regulations apply only to the activity of transmitting money or monetary value. Because an MSB license does not prohibit a business from engaging in other activities as long as it follows the necessary regulatory requirements, it imposes few limitations on potential interconnections or on the platform's overall capital position. These other activities may or may not be regulated, and hence vulnerabilities may build up in these activities. However, state MSB regulation often considers a platform's other non-money transmission activities to assess their potential impacts on the company's overall financial condition, operations, and other critical business activities and regulatory commitments as a licensed MSB.

Many large platforms in the U.S. also sometimes emphasize their regulatory status through other specific state-level regulatory regimes for entities engaged in crypto-asset activities. These state-level licenses or charters may not provide individual regulators with visibility into the activities of affiliates or subsidiaries of the entities that are licensed or chartered. However, they do create requirements for crypto-asset activities and impose prudential standards that may reduce the risk of interconnections. For example, the NYDFS "BitLicense" for entities other than those chartered under the New York Banking Law limits the scope of entities that may engage in "virtual currency" business activity and imposes capital and surety bond requirements that may vary depending on business model and risk. As of July 31, 2022, NYDFS had granted BitLicenses to 22 entities, 11 of which also held money transmitter licenses.[245] NYDFS has also granted approval for "virtual currency"

---

243 *See* Section 10.01(a), CSBS Money Transmission Modernization Act ("A licensee under this [Act] shall maintain at all times a tangible net worth of the greater of $100,000 or 3% of total assets for the first $100 million, 2% of additional assets for $100 million to $1 billion, and 0.5% of additional assets for over $1 billion.")

244 *Id.* at 10.03(a) ("A licensee shall maintain at all times permissible investments that have a market value computed in accordance with United States generally accepted accounting principles of not less than the aggregate amount of all of its outstanding money transmission obligations.")

245 NYDFS, "Virtual Currency Businesses," at https://www.dfs.ny.gov/virtual_currency_businesses.

business activities to nine limited purpose trust companies, as mentioned in part 4.2.2, Regulation of Banks', Credit Unions', and Trust Companies' Interactions with Crypto-Assets, though the limited purpose trust charter is not specific to crypto-assets. Louisiana, Nebraska, and Wyoming have also each enacted capital and surety bond or other security requirements for entities chartered or licensed in those states under crypto-asset provisions.[246]

4.5 Regulations Relating to Operational Vulnerabilities

Part 3.3.3, Operational Vulnerabilities, identified operational vulnerabilities inside the crypto-asset ecosystem.

One set of operational vulnerabilities relates to technological risks, particularly those posed by DLT and disruptions to key services. Certain regulations governing operational and technology risks may mitigate these vulnerabilities, though their effectiveness depends, in part, upon compliance by market participants. For example, an array of operational risk requirements applies to firms subject to SEC or CFTC regulations. Banks and credit unions must operate in a safe and sound manner. Codified safety and soundness standards require that banks adequately address the operational risks of their activities, including information security. The FDIC, FRB, and OCC also require banking organizations to notify the appropriate agency in the event of computer-security incidents that may materially and adversely affect the banking organization. Federal regulators are also closely monitoring cybersecurity risks at supervised firms.[247]

The current lack of technical standards complicates efforts to control for the operational risks posed by the crypto-asset ecosystem. While efforts to improve technical standards are underway,[248] the crypto-asset ecosystem generally lacks such standards, exacerbating compliance challenges and operational vulnerabilities. Due to the lack of standards, financial market participants are limited in their ability to make prudent decisions that support the integrity and safety of the markets in which they operate, potentially resulting in financial instability in the event of a disruption. Control techniques used by various crypto-asset entities may differ. The degree of internal and external auditor expertise may also affect operational risks posed by the lack of industry standards.

---

246 Louisiana's security requirement for virtual currency businesses do not apply to "regulated financial institutions," which include domestically chartered depository institutions and their subsidiaries, as well as trust companies, but excludes industrial loan companies and trust companies chartered by states without a reciprocity agreement with Louisiana. La. Stat. §§ 6:1382(13), 6:1383(C)(2). Wyoming's requirements only apply to SPDIs.

247 FRB, "Cybersecurity and Financial System Resilience Report," September 2021, at https://www.federalreserve.gov/publications/files/cybersecurity-report-202109.pdf.

248 *See* National Institute of Standards and Technology, "Blockchain," at https://www.nist.gov/blockchain.

A second set of operational vulnerabilities identified in part 3.3.3, Operational Vulnerabilities, involves concentration or procyclicality risks related to services provided by miners, validators, blockchain maintainers, other infrastructure providers, platforms, stablecoin issuers, and custody and wallet providers. The providers of these services may be subject to, though not necessarily in compliance with, requirements that would mitigate the risks of service disruptions. More broadly, to the extent that traditional financial institutions were to engage with such entities, those entities may be subject to direct or indirect scrutiny. Requirements to control operational risks generally extend to third-party relationships, as discussed in part 4.2.2, Regulation of Banks', Credit Unions', and Trust Companies' Interactions with Crypto-Assets.

Part 3.3.3, Operational Vulnerabilities, also identified a set of operational risks presented by platforms, stablecoin issuers, and custody and wallet providers. Regulation of these entities is discussed in other parts, including parts 4.4, Regulations Relating to Financial Exposures via Interconnections within the Crypto-Asset Ecosystem; 4.6, Regulation Relating to Funding Mismatches and Risks of Runs; and 5.3.2, Regulatory Arbitrage.

4.6 Regulations Relating to Funding Mismatches and Risks of Runs

Platforms

Crypto-asset platform activities may create funding mismatches and risks of runs, as discussed in part 3.3.4, Funding Mismatches and Risk of Runs.

U.S. laws and regulations include provisions designed to mitigate run risks, whether related to the possibility of rapid customer withdrawals or the loss of short-term funding more generally, as well as risks that arise from failure to custody customer assets properly. However, many crypto-asset platforms are not registered or chartered under regulatory frameworks that would address these risks.

In general, exchange and broker-dealer registration laws would require registered platforms to take certain actions to protect customer assets and, in the process, reduce the risk of runs. While broker-dealers do not accept deposits, they may rely on short-term borrowings, which create funding mismatches and make them susceptible to runs. Broker-dealers must comply with the SEC's net capital rule, which is designed to address these risks, as well as the customer protection rule, which requires segregation of customer assets, among other things. SEC rules also place limits on rehypothecation of client assets. In the context of crypto-assets, the SEC has issued guidance on the application of the customer protection rule to broker-dealers of crypto-asset securities.[249] In addition, SIPC insures up to $500,000 of assets in brokerage accounts, limited to $250,000 for cash.[250] While SIPC only insures the return of custodied assets in the event of a broker-dealer's failure and does not protect against declines in asset values, it reduces incentives for customers to run.

The regulatory framework for derivatives intermediaries such as FCMs, introducing brokers, swap dealers, major swap participants, security-based swap dealers, and major security-based swap participants, also addresses run risks. These entities are subject to minimum capital requirements, and to the extent they hold customer funds, they are also subject to segregation requirements for such funds.

Banks are subject to safety and soundness requirements designed, among other things, to address the risk of runs and to protect customer assets held in custody. In addition to capital requirements, banks must operate in a safe and sound manner, and certain banks are subject to the liquidity coverage ratio (LCR) and the net stable funding ratio (NSFR), which apply consistent and quantitative liquidity requirements.[251] The availability of federal deposit insurance mitigates risks related to runs on deposits. Separately, assets held off-balance sheet in custody—including crypto-assets—are not covered by deposit insurance. Capital and liquidity requirements also mitigate the risks of custody services.[252] In the context of crypto-assets, the OCC has released an interpretive letter discussing the application of traditional bank custody principles to crypto-assets.[253]

Some crypto-asset-specific licenses or charters also contain provisions to address funding mismatches and run risk. New York BitLicensees must hold "virtual currency" in the same amount and type as the BitLicensee stores, holds, or maintains custody or control of on behalf of another person. They are prohibited from using or encumbering virtual currency or other assets that are stored, held, or maintained, or under their custody or control, on behalf of another person, except for the

---

249 Custody of Digital Asset Securities by Special Purpose Broker-Dealers, 86 Fed. Reg. 11,627 (Feb. 2021), at https://www.sec.gov/rules/policy/2020/34-90788.pdf.

250 SIPA protections do not extend to crypto-assets that are not securities.

251 The LCR and NSFR generally apply to global systemically important bank holding companies, global systemically important depository institutions, Category II and Category III banks, Category IV Federal Reserve Board-regulated institutions with $50 billion or more in average weighted short-term wholesale funding, and covered nonbank companies. Banks engaged in digital asset activities that are not subject to these requirements would not need to comply with them, but they would still need to manage risks related to funding mismatches and runs and operate in safe and sound manner.

252 For banks that primarily engage in custody activities, regulators may impose capital and liquidity requirements that account for those specific risks, such as operational risk. *See, e.g.,* OCC 2007-21 ("Bank capital is generally used to support the bank's risk profile, business strategies, and future growth prospects and to provide a cushion against unexpected losses.")

253 *See* OCC Interpretive Letter 1170.

sale, transfer, or assignment of assets at the direction of that person. They must maintain capital in the form of cash, "virtual currency," or high-quality, highly liquid, investment-grade assets in an amount and composition that the Superintendent of NYDFS determines sufficient to ensure the BitLicensee's financial integrity given the nature of its business. Several requirements also apply to Wyoming SPDIs. SPDIs must maintain a contingency account for unexpected losses and expenses. An SPDI must maintain certain unencumbered liquid assets valued at not less than 100 percent of its depository liabilities. Non-deposit customer funds at an SPDI are not federally insured.

As noted in part 4.4, Regulations Relating to Financial Exposures via Interconnections within the Crypto-Asset Ecosystem, some platforms emphasize that they are regulated through MSB laws. These laws generally are intended to address consumer protection related to money transmission and to combat illicit finance. They are not intended to address funding mismatches outside of money transmission or risks posed by platforms custodying crypto-assets internally within omnibus accounts, particularly when commingled with platform assets. MSB laws and regulations also do not provide a general framework to address run risks of a large multi-activity financial institution.

In recognition of the growing number of platforms that custody crypto-assets, SEC staff released SAB 121 in March 2022.[254] Under SAB 121, an entity responsible for safeguarding crypto-assets for platform users should present a liability on its balance sheet to reflect its obligation to safeguard the crypto-assets held for its platform users, and recognize a corresponding asset, measured at initial recognition and each reporting date at the fair value of the crypto-assets held for its platform users. SAB 121 also clarifies the SEC staff view that platforms should provide disclosures regarding the nature and amount of crypto-assets held for users, risks involved with holding cryptographic keys, and their methods of valuing crypto-assets.

Stablecoins

Regulation that could affect run risk of stablecoins depends on the regulatory framework under which a stablecoin issuer operates. To date, stablecoin issuers in the U.S. have operated under a number of different regulatory regimes, as well as outside of or in non-compliance with existing regulatory regimes.

Some stablecoin issuers in the U.S. have noted that they are subject to regulation as MSBs. As described above with respect to platforms, MSB regulation is generally intended to address consumer protection related to money transmission activities and illicit finance.

---

254 SEC, SAB 121, March 31, 2022, at https://www.sec.gov/oca/staff-accounting-bulletin-121. SAB 121 provides staff-level interpretive guidance for existing accounting rules. It applies to SEC filers, including entities whose registration statements are not yet effective, and certain other entities.

Some stablecoin issuers are regulated by NYDFS. In June 2022, NYDFS issued stablecoin guidance that would apply to stablecoins issued by New York-chartered limited purpose trust companies and BitLicensees.[255] The guidance includes requirements related to reserve assets, redemption policies, management of liquidity risks, and regular attestations. This guidance does not apply to stablecoins listed by NYDFS-regulated entities but issued by entities that NYDFS does not regulate. Nebraska has also enacted a requirement that a digital asset depository must maintain unencumbered liquid assets that equal the value of its outstanding stablecoins.

Some regulation of stablecoins relevant for run risks has also come through legal agreements with specific companies. For example, New York reached a settlement in 2021 with Tether, the largest global stablecoin.[256] Among other items, the settlement required Tether to cease trading with New York persons or entities and to publish information quarterly on its asset holdings, somewhat decreasing opacity about the stablecoin.

Some stablecoin issuers have explored the possibility of obtaining bank charters. All IDIs are subject to extensive banking regulations that help mitigate the risk of runs.[257] In general, banks must operate in a safe and sound manner and are subject to comprehensive supervision, including for liquidity risk.[258] As noted above, certain banks are subject to the LCR and the NSFR. In addition, IDIs offer deposits that are insured, subject to limits, and have access to emergency liquidity and Federal Reserve services.[259] Depositors whose deposit accounts are fully insured have little

---

255 NYDFS, "Guidance on the Issuance of U.S. Dollar-Backed Stablecoins," June 8, 2022, at https://www.dfs.ny.gov/industry_guidance/industry_letters/il20220608_issuance_stablecoins.

256 *In the Matter of Investigation by Letitia James, Attorney General of the State of New York, of iFinex Inc., BFXNA Inc., BFXWW Inc., Tether Holdings Limited, Tether Operations Limited, Tether Limited, and Tether International Limited*, February 17, 2021, at https://ag.ny.gov/sites/default/files/2021.02.17_-_settlement_agreement_-_execution_version.b-t_signed-c2_oag_signed.pdf.

257 As discussed above, national trust banks and state trust companies often do not accept deposits and, therefore, face different liquidity risks. The OCC may tailor requirements for national banks to address the risks presented by the institution's business model. *See* OCC Bulletin 2007-21, June 26, 2007, at https://www.occ.gov/news-issuances/bulletins/2007/bulletin-2007-21.html. A stablecoin may be subject to different liquidity risks depending on how its underlying reserves are structured.

258 For a detailed discussion of these risks, supervisory expectations, and examination procedures, see, for example, FDIC, Risk Management Manual of Examination Policies Section 6.1, October 2019, at https://www.fdic.gov/regulations/safety/manual/section6-1.pdf. OCC, Comptroller's Handbook, Liquidity, August 16, 2021, at https://www.occ.treas.gov/publications-and-resources/publications/comptrollers-handbook/files/liquidity/pub-ch-liquidity.pdf. FRB, "Liquidity Risk Management," at https://www.federalreserve.gov/supervisionreg/topics/liquidity_risk.htm.

259 PWG, FDIC, and OCC, *Report on Stablecoins*, November 2021, https://home.treasury.gov/system/files/136/StableCoinReport_Nov1_508.pdf.

incentive to run. Run risks may also be mitigated by capital adequacy standards and other loss-reserving standards instituted by federal bank regulators.[260]

The PWG Report discusses risks of stablecoin arrangements, the lack of a consistent regulatory framework, and the benefits of limiting stablecoin issuance and related activities to IDIs. It also notes that "[d]epending on their structure, stablecoins, or certain parts of stablecoin arrangements, may be securities, commodities, and/or derivatives. Moreover, much of the trading, lending, and borrowing activity currently fueled by stablecoins on [crypto-asset] trading platforms and within DeFi similarly may constitute securities and/or derivatives transactions that must be conducted in compliance with federal securities laws and the CEA, including applicable regulations. To the extent that a given stablecoin activity falls within the jurisdiction of the SEC and/or CFTC, it must be conducted in compliance with applicable provisions of the federal securities laws and/or the CEA."[261]

Regulatory efforts to reduce run risk have a long history. Box F discusses this and other aspects of regulatory history relevant for crypto-asset activities in more detail.

Box F: Crypto-Assets and the History of American Financial Regulation

The financial regulatory challenges posed by the rapid growth of crypto-assets evoke analogies to episodes in American financial history in which new innovations or institutional arrangements rapidly changed the American financial system. These episodes highlight the importance of robust financial regulation, key elements of which were developed in response to the episodes described in this box. The rapid growth of banks during the so-called "free banking" period of the mid-19th century highlights the benefits of regulation that addresses the financial stability issues posed by competing private assets that attempt to provide functions and attributes of money and is useful to consider in the context of crypto-assets such as stablecoins. The rapid expansion of retail securities markets in the 1920s highlights the vital importance of federal securities laws enacted beginning in the 1930s and that apply to securities traded in crypto-asset markets. Finally, the development of derivatives markets leading up to the 2007-2009 financial crisis emphasizes the dangers posed by complex and opaque interdependencies, often with hidden leverage, which is relevant to interconnections in crypto-asset markets.

Taken together, a broad view of financial history underscores the importance of a technologically neutral policy that is attentive to the risks that new technologies, products, and other developments pose. Such a policy supports and guides—but does not try to direct—the process of financial innovation.

---

260 Loss reserving standards (e.g., allowances for credit losses) also help ensure that banks have the capacity to absorb some level of anticipated and unexpected losses while maintaining solvency. Federal capital adequacy standards include both risk-based and non-risk-weighted leverage requirements. Qualifying community banking organizations may elect to use only the community bank leverage ratio framework.

261 PWG, FDIC, and OCC, *Report on Stablecoins*, (November 2021), p. 11, at https://home.treasury.gov/news/press-releases/jy0454.

Free Banking Era

The free banking era is generally considered to be the period from 1837—when a proto-central bank, the Second Bank of the United States, was dissolved—until the creation of the national banking system in 1863 amidst the Civil War. During this period, the federal government had little footprint in the banking system as it did not charter or regulate banks. State-level regulation of banking varied widely.[262] The result was fragmentation in the banking and monetary systems. Currency during the free banking era consisted of bank notes, that is, liabilities of individual banks payable in gold or silver if presented at the issuing bank. Unlike deposits, bank notes circulated as bearer instruments, similar to cash today. As many as 1,500 currencies circulated at any one time.[263] This proliferation, under different state-level regulatory regimes, of multiple competing private assets attempting to provide some functions and attributes of money bears some resemblance to crypto-assets such as stablecoins, issuers of which do not have a consistent or comprehensive regulatory framework or that have at times purported to be outside the regulatory perimeter.

Banking regulation from the free banking era offers a strong lesson on the importance of robust regulation for crypto-assets. Research on the free banking era has found that strong regulation of the collateral backing bank notes was a key factor in preventing runs and preserving the financial condition of banks. The majority of banks that failed did so in states where banks were allowed or required to back their notes with risky bonds and during times of declines in those bond prices.[264] In response to this poor experience and federal financing needs during the Civil War, federal law authorized the Comptroller of the Currency to charter national banks that would issue bank notes backed by U.S. Treasury instruments. As the national banking system developed over the late 19th and early 20th centuries, the backing requirement addressed one major source of instability in the banking system compared to the free banking era and created a uniform national currency. However, bank runs continued to be a problem, and banking regulation continued to evolve, especially after the Great Depression.

Another strong lesson from the free banking era is that regulators have an important role in addressing fraud and inefficiency that can arise amidst the rapid development of multiple competing private assets intended to function as currencies. Fraud was common during the free banking era. For example, schemes emerged inventing a nonexistent bank with a name similar to an existing bank or altering the notes issued by a real bank.[265] In

---

262 At the state level, banking entry tended to be highly restricted in the early 19th century. Before general incorporation laws, banking charters were largely available only through acts of state legislatures. On the whole, financial historians view liberalization of banking charters as desirable in order to increase the capacity of the financial sector and to support the industrialization of the U.S.

263 Gorton, Gary, "The Development of Opacity in U.S. Banking," Working Paper, 2013, at https://www.nber.org/papers/w19540.

264 Jaremski, Matthew, "Free bank failures: Risky bonds versus undiversified portfolios," *Journal of Money, Credit and Banking,* vol. 42 no. 8, 2010, pp. 1565-1587, at https://www.jstor.org/stable/40925703.

265 Weber, Warren, "Banknote Exchange Rates in the Antebellum United States," Working Paper, 2002, at https://www.minneapolisfed.org/research/wp/wp623.pdf.

response, an industry arose to evaluate bank notes. Merchants would consult printed catalogs of all known bank notes and apply discounts suggested by those catalogs to the face value of bank notes. Newspapers carried similar lists. Research has found that those discounts tended to be smaller if the quality of the bonds backing the notes was strong, if the likelihood of redemption was high, if banks were located nearby, so the cost of travel to redeem was low, and if banks were well-established.[266] Like state bank notes, stablecoin prices in the secondary market fluctuate depending on a variety of factors, including perceptions of risk about the future likelihood of redemption.

The Early 20th Century Growth of the Retail Securities Market

Certain crypto-assets have been or may currently be offered and sold in transactions that are not in compliance with federal or state securities laws. This results in securities being offered, sold, and traded without required disclosures or market oversight. Such instances of non-compliance evoke securities markets before the enactment of federal or state securities laws in the first half of the 20th century. Indeed, the growth in crypto-asset market participation, especially at the retail level, mirrors the mushrooming of ownership of corporate stock in the United States from less than one million individuals in 1910 to more than 10 million by the early 1930s.[267] The growth of a retail securities market was a major change in the American financial structure. In response, the passage of state securities laws beginning in the 1910s and federal securities laws beginning in the 1930s created significant legal guardrails around the ways in which financial products could be offered for sale to the public and on the way such products could be traded.

Pump-and-dump schemes in crypto-asset markets evoke abusive practices from this period of financial history, such as when stock pools temporarily manipulated and drove up stock prices long enough for insiders to cash out.[268] Ponzi schemes in crypto-asset markets are named for Charles Ponzi, who was convicted at the federal level only of mail fraud, given the lack of federal securities laws at the time. Super Bowl advertisements designed to draw retail investors into crypto-asset markets are reminiscent of the marketing of securities toward inexperienced retail investors in the 1920s.[269] Just as unregistered securities offerings leave crypto-asset investors vulnerable to confusion about what products they are buying, the lack of securities regulation in the 1920s led

266 Gorton, Gary, Chase P. Ross, and Sharon Y. Ross, "Making Money" Working paper, 2022, at https://www.nber.org/papers/w29710.

267 Hilt, Eric, Matthew S. Jaremski, and Wendy Rahn, "When Uncle Sam Introduced Main Street to Wall Street: Liberty Bonds and the Transformation of American Finance" *Journal of Financial Economics* vol. 145 no. 1, 2022, at https://www.sciencedirect.com/science/article/abs/pii/S0304405X21003135.

268 Pontecorvo, Giulio, "Investment Banking and Security Speculation in the Late 1920's," *Business History Review,* vol. 32, no. 2, 1958, pp. 166-191, at https://www.jstor.org/stable/pdf/3111701.pdf.

269 Wiggers, Tyler and Adam Ashcraft, *"Defaults and Losses on Commercial Real Estate Bonds during the Great Depression Era,"* Federal Reserve Bank of New York Staff Report no. 544, 2012, at https://www.newyorkfed.org/research/economists/medialibrary/media/research/staff_reports/sr544.pdf.

to similar confusion.[270] These historical similarities indicate the highest importance of securities laws that protect investors, especially in the context of growing retail participation.

Derivatives Market

Derivatives markets grew very rapidly in the decades prior to the 2007-2009 financial crisis. Although providing some innovations in risk management, these new derivative markets also contributed to or propagated the financial crisis. Through credit default swaps, the financial system built up a complex and opaque set of interconnections that amplified mortgage market shocks widely throughout the financial system. Over-the-counter markets, which Congress largely exempted from regulation until the passage of the Dodd-Frank Act, were also characterized by complexity and opacity, contributing to excessive risk taking, hidden leverage, and a lack of clarity about the ultimate distribution of risks.[271] The growth of crypto-asset activities carries reminders of these experiences. Like derivatives markets, crypto-assets markets have experienced rapid growth, and crypto-asset proponents believe the innovations can bring a suite of benefits for the financial system. These activities have also created several complex and opaque interdependencies. Ostensibly "decentralized" platforms are an example of choices by market participants to pursue operations that can obscure the identities of counterparties and information about the ultimate distribution of risks. Unlike derivatives markets in the lead-up to the financial crisis, Congress has not exempted crypto-assets from regulation, though many crypto-asset firms have sought to avoid the existing regulatory system.

4.7 Regulations Relating to Leverage

Regulatory guardrails on leverage obtained by crypto-assets market participants vary substantially across the forums in which leverage is obtained.

In securities markets, the Federal Reserve's Regulations T, U, and X govern extensions of credit in crypto-assets that are securities and establish margin limits on securities positions. Exchanges, SROs, national securities associations, and creditors may impose heightened requirements on extensions of credit by registered broker-dealers.

In margined commodity, futures, or derivative products, significant guardrails exist for leverage embedded in such products and traded on regulated exchanges. The amount of leverage an investor can take on in a particular contract is limited by exchange rules or by the exchange's clearinghouse. More generally, the extent

---

270 Janette Rutterford, "Learning from one another's mistakes: investment trusts in the UK and the US, 1868-1940," *Financial History Review,* 2009, pp. 157-181, at https://www.cambridge.org/core/journals/financial-history-review/article/abs/learning-from-one-anothers-mistakes-investment-trusts-in-the-uk-and-the-us-18681940/52AAAAD409A7F49C0E9AFD221AD07D2D.

271 FSOC, *2011 Annual Report,* p. 25, at https://home.treasury.gov/system/files/261/FSOCAR2011.pdf.

of leverage is subject to oversight by the CFTC and the SEC, as applicable.[272] In addition, intermediaries can, at their discretion, charge their customers a higher margin requirement than required by the exchange, resulting in lower leverage. The CFTC has also enforced the prohibition on off-exchange retail commodity transactions, described in part 4.2.4, Regulations Relating to Financial Products. For example, in September 2021 the CFTC ordered a $1.25 million civil monetary penalty from a platform for illegally offering margined retail commodity transactions in assets such as Bitcoin outside a DCM and for failing to register as an FCM.[273]

To the extent that leveraged transactions do not take place on registered exchanges or are not handled by registered intermediaries, such products may not be bounded by comprehensive guardrails with respect to leverage. As a result, leverage may be in excess of what a prudential regulator would deem appropriate. Poor auditing or disclosure standards may also create situations in which leverage is higher than market participants intended or perceive. Offshore platforms provide opportunities for very high leverage outside of the U.S. regulatory perimeter. Some platforms have also offered very high leverage to U.S. customers and attempted to evade applicable laws and regulations by operating in an ostensibly decentralized manner, though such characterizations do not have legal effect. Shocks to highly leveraged market participants outside the United States may impact U.S. customers because of the cross-border nature of crypto-asset markets.

Guardrails on the leverage obtained through loans depends largely on the type of regulation to which the lending institution is subjected. Large platforms appear to be engaging in some prime brokerage-type activity and making loans to miners, and such loans are likely not subjected to comprehensive guardrails in the absence of greater regulation of those platforms in practice.

If banks were to engage in lending related to crypto-asset activities, prudential regulation and supervision could affect the amount of leverage they would provide. Safe and sound underwriting of loans by banks may limit the extent of leverage. For example, banks assess the value of collateral and the loan purpose pursuant to the codified interagency safety and soundness standards, which could affect the availability and terms of any funding provided by a bank.

---

272 The Federal Reserve delegated its authority to establish margin requirements for security futures products to the SEC and the CFTC. Letter from Jennifer J. Johnson, Secretary of the Board, FRB, to James E. Newsome, Acting Chairman, CFTC, and Laura S. Unger, Acting Chairman, SEC (March 6, 2001).

273 CFTC, Release No. 8433-21, "CFTC Imposes A $1.25 Million Penalty against Kraken for Offering Illegal Off-Exchange Digital Asset Trading and Failing to Register as Required," September 28, 2021, at https://www.cftc.gov/PressRoom/PressReleases/8433-21.

4.8 FSOC Authorities

As noted in the preamble to this report and consistent with its statutory purposes and duties, the FSOC seeks to identify and respond to vulnerabilities in the U.S. financial system so that abrupt and unpredictable shocks to economic or financial conditions do not impair the ability of the financial system to provide needed services, including the clearing of payments, the provision of liquidity, and the availability of credit.

Under the Dodd-Frank Act, the FSOC has specific authorities to promote those goals that could be applied to crypto-asset activities or entities. These authorities include the designation of nonbank financial companies, financial market utilities, and payment, clearing or settlement activities. Designation would subject these entities or activities to additional supervision and regulation intended to address the financial stability vulnerabilities they present. To date, the FSOC has not used its designation authorities for crypto-asset activities or entities. The FSOC may also provide for more stringent regulation of a financial activity by issuing recommendations to the primary financial regulatory agencies to apply new or heightened standards and safeguards for a financial activity or practice conducted by bank holding companies or nonbank financial companies.

5 Council Recommendations

The Council finds that crypto-asset activities could pose risks to the stability of the U.S. financial system if their interconnections with the traditional financial system or their overall scale were to grow without being paired with appropriate regulation, including enforcement of the existing regulatory structure. This part of the report details the Council's recommendations to ensure appropriate regulation of crypto-asset activities.

The Council notes that large parts of the crypto-asset ecosystem are covered by the existing regulatory structure. In applying these existing authorities, the Council recommends that its members take into consideration a set of principles detailed in part 5.1. The Council also emphasizes the importance of continued enforcement of existing rules and regulations, as discussed in part 5.2.

The Council has identified three gaps in the regulation of crypto-asset activities in the United States:

- limited direct federal oversight of the spot market for crypto-assets that are not securities;
- opportunities for regulatory arbitrage; and
- whether vertically integrated market structures can or should be accommodated under existing laws and regulations.

To address these gaps, the Council recommends the passage of legislation providing for rulemaking authority for federal financial regulators over the spot market for crypto-assets that are not securities (part 5.3.1); steps to address regulatory arbitrage including coordination, legislation regarding risks posed by stablecoins, legislation relating to regulators' authorities to have visibility into, and otherwise supervise, the activities of all of the affiliates and subsidiaries of crypto-asset entities, and appropriate service provider regulation (part 5.3.2); and study of potential vertical integration by crypto-asset firms (part 5.3.3). Finally, the Council recommends bolstering its members' capacities related to data (part 5.4) and to the analysis, monitoring, supervision, and regulation of crypto-asset activities (part 5.5).

5.1 Consideration of Regulatory Principles

Recommendation 1: As the crypto-asset market continues to develop, and in recognition of the potential for increases in scale and interconnections with the traditional financial system, the Council recommends that its member agencies consider these general principles in their deliberations about the applicability of current authorities:

- same activity, same risk, same regulatory outcome;
- technological neutrality;

- leveraging existing authorities where appropriate;
- transparency in technology, including through potential future adoption and implementation of federal agency SBOM requirements by industry;
- addressing financial stability risks before they impair the economy;
- monitoring mechanisms through which crypto-assets could become more interconnected with the traditional financial system or increase in overall scale;
- bringing transparency to opaque areas, including through disclosures and documentation of key issues such as interconnectedness;
- prioritizing timely and orderly transaction processing and legally binding settlement;
- facilitating price discovery and fostering market integrity; and
- obtaining, and sharing with other agencies, relevant market data from the crypto-asset market.

5.2 Continued Enforcement

Recommendation 2: The Council recommends that agencies continue to enforce existing rules and regulations, including but not limited to product, exchange, and other applicable market participant registration requirements; banking laws; anti-fraud laws; securities laws; commodities and derivatives laws; anti-money laundering laws; sanctions; and consumer and investor protection laws. The Council reiterates that bank and credit union regulators expect that banks and credit unions that engage in crypto-asset activities do so in a safe and sound manner and in compliance with applicable laws and regulations.

5.3 Addressing Regulatory Gaps

Though the existing regulatory system covers large parts of the crypto-asset ecosystem, this report identifies three gaps in the regulation of crypto-asset activities in the United States.

5.3.1 Regulation of the Spot Market for Crypto-Assets That Are Not Securities

The Council has identified a gap related to the regulation of the spot market for crypto-assets that are not securities. Box G describes this gap in detail.

Box G: The Regulation of the Spot Market for Crypto-Assets That Are Not Securities

U.S. law provides for limited direct federal oversight of spot markets for crypto-assets that are not securities, i.e., the market in which trades occur for Bitcoin and possibly other crypto-assets that are not securities. As a result, those markets may not feature robust rules and regulations designed to ensure orderly and transparent trading, to prevent conflicts of interest and market manipulation, and to protect investors and the economy more broadly. Indeed, U.S. regulators have found possible sources of fraud and manipulation in the spot Bitcoin market.[274]

The spot markets for crypto-assets that are not securities provide relatively fewer protections for retail investors compared to other financial markets that have significant retail participation. For example, the spot market for Bitcoin, as well as other crypto-assets, is characterized by a high proportion of retail investors speculating on price movements (see part 3.3.1, Crypto-Asset Prices). In contrast, speculation in physical commodity markets is more confined to the regulated derivatives markets. Physical commodity spot markets have traditionally been dominated by wholesalers and large financial institutions rather than retail participants, who generally do not take delivery of a physical commodity in bulk in order to speculate on its price.

In addition, crypto-asset platforms in the spot market for non-security crypto-assets engage in practices that are commonly subjected to greater regulation in other financial markets. In particular, to accommodate the large number of speculative participants in crypto-asset markets, including retail investors, a number of crypto-asset platforms operate order book-style markets, a practice that is not widespread in retail-accessible physical commodity markets. In similarly structured financial markets, trading rules apply related to practices of trade execution and settlement to ensure fairness and transparency and to limit abusive trading practices more generally.

Many crypto-asset platforms also custody customer crypto-assets. These platforms typically are not subject to the same regulatory treatment as institutions that play a similar custodial and fiduciary role for retail investors, such as banks and regulated market intermediaries. As detailed in part 3, Financial Stability Risks, though, these platforms are prone to unique operational vulnerabilities and there have been multiple demonstrated incidents of platforms losing or misappropriating customer funds.

Finally, the technical design choices of crypto-assets allows them to be transferred easily across borders, ultimately making these markets inherently global in nature. Such choices heighten the need for domestic investor protections and AML/CFT.

In addition, while the CFTC has broad authorities related to derivatives transactions in crypto-assets that are not securities, U.S. financial regulation of spot markets for such crypto-assets is limited to certain specific authorities. Non-security crypto-assets have been regulated by institutions like FinCEN since 2013, the regulatory coverage of which is a matter of facts and circumstances. In addition, certain transactions that are conducted on a leveraged or margined basis, known as "retail commodity transactions," are treated as futures transactions and must occur on a CFTC-regulated exchange.[275] To not be

---

274 SEC, Release No. 34-95180, June 29, 2022, at https://www.sec.gov/rules/sro/nysearca/2022/34-95180.pdf.

275 The CFTC has issued guidance on what is a derivative transaction and what is a spot transaction in the context of crypto-assets. CFTC, Retail Commodity Transactions Involving Virtual Currency, 82 Fed. Reg. 60335 (Dec. 20, 2017), at https://www.govinfo.gov/content/pkg/FR-2017-12-20/pdf/2017-27421.pdf.

considered a retail commodity transaction, spot transactions must involve the actual delivery of the associated commodity within 28 days (or such other longer period as the CFTC may establish by rule or regulation). In cases in which there is actual delivery within 28 days or in which the transactions are not on a leveraged or margined basis, the CFTC's commodity spot market authority is generally limited to antifraud and anti-manipulation authorities. Finally, entities that are engaged in the spot market for non-security crypto-assets may be required to comply with certain federal and state money transmission and anti-money laundering laws.

Significant market integrity and investor protection issues may persist because of the limited direct federal oversight of these spot markets, due to abusive trading practices, inadequate protections for custodied assets, or other practices. Increased interconnections between this market and traditional financial institutions could pose financial stability vulnerabilities. In addition, if the scale of crypto-asset activities were to increase rapidly, these issues could pose financial stability issues regardless of interconnections with the traditional financial system.

Recommendation 3: To address this regulatory gap, the Council recommends that Congress pass legislation that provides for explicit rulemaking authority for federal financial regulators over the spot market for crypto-assets that are not securities. The Council recommends that this rulemaking authority should not interfere with or weaken market regulators' current jurisdictional remits. The rulemaking authority should cover a range of subjects, including but not limited to conflicts of interest; abusive trading practices; public trade reporting requirements; recordkeeping; governance standards; cybersecurity requirements; customer asset segregation; capital and margin; custody, settlement, and clearing; orderly trading; transparency; any further anti-fraud authorities that may be necessary; investor protection; dispute resolution; operating norms; and a general authority to address unanticipated additional issues that may arise. Legislation should provide for enforcement and examination authority to ensure compliance with these rules.

5.3.2 Regulatory Arbitrage

The Council has identified a regulatory gap relating to regulatory arbitrage. Box H describes this gap in detail.

Box H: Regulatory Arbitrage

Currently, crypto-asset entities do not have a consistent or comprehensive regulatory framework and can take advantage of gaps in the regulatory system and engage in regulatory arbitrage. Opportunities for regulatory arbitrage arise when the same activity can be carried out lawfully under more than one regulatory framework. Regulatory arbitrage therefore differs from noncompliance with laws that permit certain activities only under specific regulatory frameworks.

Crypto-asset firms may prefer to operate under different regulations that arise from varying core principles across state and federal charters; across state regulatory regimes; across

U.S.-based and international regulation; and across the regulations applied to entities and their third-party service providers. They also may choose different regulatory regimes for different affiliates or subsidiaries. In such cases, the regulatory system for crypto-assets may not provide any single regulator with a comprehensive view of a firm as a whole or its relationships with third-party service providers.

Regulatory arbitrage may have a wide range of financial stability implications if activities that bear the same risks are subject to different rules or if firms can operate in a manner that prevents regulators from assessing the totality of an entity's risks. For example, the riskiness of an entity's capital position—and therefore the risks that an entity poses to its counterparties via interconnections—is challenging to fully assess without information on risks taken across all of that entity's affiliates or subsidiaries. As another example, risk of runs can persist if entities engage in a regulatory race to the bottom, seeking to operate under whatever regulatory framework places the fewest limitations on funding mismatches.

Regulatory arbitrage considerations may apply to a range of entities in the crypto-asset ecosystem, including stablecoins and crypto-asset platforms.

Stablecoin issuers may be engaging in regulatory arbitrage. Some stablecoin issuers in the U.S. note that they have received state-level MSB licenses and have registered as MSBs with FinCEN, though state-level MSB regulation is generally only intended to address consumer protection related narrowly to money transmission activities and FinCEN's regulations focus on combating illicit finance. Stablecoin issuers could receive limited purpose trust charters or special crypto-asset charters or licenses at the state level. If a stablecoin issuer has affiliates as part of a broader crypto-asset business, neither MSB licenses nor trust or state-level crypto-asset charters or licenses necessarily provide a single regulator with visibility into the activities of those affiliates or the business as a whole. Other stablecoin issuers in the United States have sought banking charters, and some existing banks have announced their aspirations to issue stablecoins or tokenized deposits. To date, however, stablecoin issuers have not operated through full-service bank charters, which could raise novel risks. Other stablecoin issuers operate outside the United States altogether or may operate domestically while in non-compliance with the U.S. regulatory structure, including potentially securities laws. The level of compliance of such stablecoin issuers with laws relating to illicit finance is unclear.[276]

Crypto-asset activities that include payment services, potentially including stablecoin activities, may operate under a number of different regulatory regimes. In general, the U.S. lacks a regulator with plenary authority over retail payment systems.[277] If a particular crypto-asset entity or arrangement were to gain a dominant role in payments, clearing, and settlement, potential disruption could pose broader risk to the financial system.

---

276 Stablecoin issuers may interact with permissionless blockchains to create or "mint" or transfer stablecoins on permissionless blockchains. These issuers may be paying miners who are sanctioned persons or located in comprehensively sanctioned jurisdictions through the payment of transactions fees. One crypto-asset analytics firm estimated that in 2021, 4.5% of all Bitcoin mining took place in a single sanctioned nation state.

277 *See* United States Department of the Treasury, *The Future of Money and Payments,* September 2022, at https://home.treasury.gov/system/files/136/Future-of-Money-and-Payments.pdf. That report recommends the establishment of a federal framework for payments regulation to protect users and the financial system, while supporting responsible innovations in payments.

Crypto-asset platforms may also be engaging in regulatory arbitrage. As noted above, though, certain activities conducted by crypto-asset platforms may constitute noncompliance with applicable existing law, which is distinct from regulatory arbitrage. For example, crypto-asset platforms operating in the United States may be subject to, and non-compliant with, registration requirements if they facilitate trading of securities or commodities derivatives, depending on the facts and circumstances of the products they support. Regulatory frameworks remain applicable to crypto-asset platforms and activities regardless of any characterization or assertion of "decentralization." Many platforms could be described as universal crypto-asset financial institutions, providing a wide assortment of financial services to their customers across their different subsidiaries and affiliates. A platform's subsidiaries or affiliates may operate under different regulatory regimes depending on the activities in which they engage. Certain charters or licenses, such as MSB licenses and certain trust or state-level crypto-asset charters or licenses, may not provide a single regulator with the ability to see activities at a platform's other affiliates or subsidiaries, unless they are owned or controlled by a depository institution holding company subject to Federal Reserve supervision. In addition, platforms may operate in the U.S. while their affiliates may be subjected to different overseas regulation.

Regulatory arbitrage by crypto-asset firms may impact existing financial institutions. Crypto-asset firms may provide financial services that resemble services provided by banks, traditional securities intermediaries, or other financial institutions, but without being subject to, or in compliance with, the same standards and obligations. Traditional financial firms that are subject to more stringent rules and regulations could face a competitive disadvantage when crypto-asset firms engage in similar activities at a lower regulatory cost. Crypto-asset firms may also obtain competitive benefits and undermine traditional institutions by failing to comply with applicable regulations, although non-compliant firms run significant risks by operating as such. In addition, crypto-asset firms that rely on traditional financial institutions may expose those institutions to crypto-asset-related risks.

To address this regulatory gap and facilitate a level playing field among entities that engage in similar activities, the Council is making the following recommendations.

Recommendation 4: The Council recommends that regulators continue to coordinate with each other in the supervision of crypto-asset entities, such as stablecoins issuers or crypto-asset platforms, particularly in cases where different entities with similar activities may be subject to different regulatory regimes or when no one regulator has visibility across all affiliates, subsidiaries, and service providers of an entity. Coordination across regulatory agencies is a typical feature of American financial regulatory history in response to dispersed authorities and can help address issues related to regulatory arbitrage or the lack of a single regulator having visibility across all of an entity's affiliates. Regulators should also coordinate with law enforcement where appropriate. There may be practical challenges to enforcement if market participants are not readily identifiable, or if activities lack linkages with traditional financial institutions or markets that could otherwise facilitate regulatory oversight. There may also be practical challenges given the global reach of crypto-asset markets.

Recommendation 5: The Council recommends that Congress pass legislation that would create a comprehensive federal prudential framework for stablecoin issuers that also addresses the associated market integrity, investor and consumer protection, and payment system risks, including for entities that perform services critical to the functioning of the stablecoin arrangement. This legislation should address the financial stability risks of stablecoins in line with the principles in recommendation 1. The Council recommends that federal and state regulators coordinate on the supervision of stablecoin issuers as appropriate. The Council remains prepared to consider steps available to it to address such risks related to stablecoins in the event comprehensive legislation is not enacted.

Recommendation 6: Crypto-asset entities' operations and organizational structures may result in having different regulatory regimes for different affiliates or subsidiaries. As a result, in some cases, no single regulator may have a comprehensive view of such entities as a whole and their crypto-asset activities. The Council therefore recommends that Congress develop legislation that would create authority for regulators to have visibility into, and otherwise supervise, the activities of all of the affiliates and subsidiaries of crypto-asset entities, in cases in which regulators do not already possess such authority. Such authority would apply regardless of any characterization or assertion of a crypto-asset entity's "decentralization." The Council recommends that this legislation include authority for regulators to address regulatory arbitrage in a coordinated manner. This authority could cover, for example, restrictions on entity and affiliate activities; capital and liquidity requirements across a crypto-asset entity and all of its affiliates and subsidiaries; safety and soundness; cyber and data security practices, including third-party risk management; licensing, applications, and charters; data and disclosures; competition; and supervision, examination, and enforcement.

Recommendation 7: The Council recommends that the FDIC, FRB, OCC, and state bank regulators use their existing authorities, as appropriate, to review services provided to banks by crypto-asset service providers and other entities in the crypto-asset arena. The Council also recommends that, as they gain experience in examining crypto-asset services, the FDIC, FRB, OCC, and state bank regulators continue to evaluate whether their existing authorities are sufficient. The Council also recommends that Congress pass legislation that ensures the FHFA, NCUA, and other relevant agencies have adequate examination and enforcement authorities to oversee such entities and third-party service providers more generally.

5.3.3 Markets or Activities Featuring Direct Retail Access

The Council has identified a regulatory gap relating to markets or activities featuring direct retail access. Box I describes this gap in more detail.

Box I: Markets or Activities Featuring Direct Retail Access

The current framework of markets regulation is generally structured around the requirement or presumption that markets are accessed by retail customers through intermediaries such as broker-dealers or futures commission merchants (FCMs). Those intermediaries perform many important functions, such as processing transactions, acting as agent and obtaining best execution for customers, extending credit, managing custody of customer assets, ensuring compliance with federal regulations, and guaranteeing performance of contracts. As a result of the special role these intermediaries play in traditional market structures, they are subject to unique regulations often focused on customer protections, such as regulations around conflicts of interest, suitability, best execution, segregation of funds, disclosures, and fitness standards for employees.

Recently, however, a number of firms have proposed to offer vertically integrated services so that retail customers can directly access markets.[278] These arrangements are also sometimes known as non-intermediated, in reference to retail customers placing orders directly to an exchange, rather than through an intermediary such as a broker-dealer or an FCM, that performs certain functions.[279] Some overseas crypto-asset platforms already feature vertically integrated structures. Vertical integration is in general distinct from decentralization, and vertical integration could, in principle, be applied to either a centralized or purportedly decentralized platform.

Financial stability implications may arise from vertically integrated platforms' approaches to managing risk arising from the leverage or credit they offer. The lack of traditional intermediaries to extend and manage credit often leads these platforms to conduct mark to market settlement cycles on a very frequent basis, as often as multiple times a minute. In some cases, the platform liquidates participants' under-margined positions based on each new price rather than making margin calls through an intermediary. This type of risk management can effectively reduce risk to the trading platform by removing under-margined positions quickly rather than allowing risk to build during the time between settlement cycles, which typically occurs once a day in the intermediated model without vertical integration. However, this practice of automatically closing out customer positions creates the potential for cascading liquidations and reduced capacity for human intervention during periods of stress, as discussed in part 3.3.5, Leverage. In addition, automatic liquidations during short time horizons and outside of traditional business hours heighten the importance of price integrity at all times, and the importance of monitoring for, preventing, and policing fraud and manipulation.

Direct exposure by retail investors to rapid liquidations of this kind also raises investor and consumer protection issues. Platforms dealing directly with retail investors would need to ensure the provision of adequate disclosures, responsibilities otherwise taken on by intermediaries. The vertically integrated model presents conflicts of interest that could result in incentives to liquidate customer positions.

---

278 CFTC, "CFTC Announces Staff Roundtable Discussion on Non-intermediation," May 25, 2022, at https://www.cftc.gov/PressRoom/Events/opaeventstaffroundtable052522.

279 Other entities may still act as intermediaries between customers and such platforms, including miners and validators.

Recommendation 8: The Council recommends that member agencies assess the impact of vertical integration (i.e., direct access to markets by retail customers) on conflicts of interest and market volatility, and whether vertically integrated market structures can or should be accommodated under existing laws and regulations.

5.4 Ensuring Regulation Is Informed by Appropriate Data

The crypto-asset ecosystem is characterized by opacity that creates challenges for the assessment of financial stability risks. Collection and sharing of data, as appropriate, could help reduce this opacity.

Recommendation 9: The Council recommends a coordinated government-wide approach to data and to the analysis, monitoring, supervision, and regulation of crypto-asset activities. The Council recommends that member agencies consider the use of available data collection powers in order to facilitate assessments of the financial risks related to crypto-assets, as part of data sharing and coordination efforts among the members. The Council will continue to work with its members to coordinate efforts, as appropriate, to address data gaps related to crypto-assets, including prioritizing data sets and coordinating data acquisition, in order to avoid duplication of efforts and facilitate the improvement and coordinated use of data across Council members.

5.5 Building Regulatory Capacity and Expertise

By building capacity and expertise, Council members can accelerate their understanding of crypto-asset-related financial risks and take necessary steps to ensure the resilience of the financial system to such risks.

Recommendation 10: The Council will continue to develop its ability to monitor risks posed by crypto-assets. The Council recommends that, consistent with their budget processes and mandates, Council members continue to build their capacity to analyze and monitor crypto-asset activities and allocate sufficient resources to do so. The Council recommends that members continue to prioritize investments and efforts to build out enforcement capacity related to crypto-asset activities, including coordinated enforcement of common policies across members, state regulators, law enforcement, and state Attorneys General as appropriate. The Council also recommends that Congress appropriate necessary resources to member agencies for supervision and regulation of crypto-asset activities. The Council recommends that members continue to add or train staff and engage with government, private-sector, and academic partners to build expertise related to rapidly evolving technological innovation in the crypto-asset space, including capacity to analyze publicly available blockchain data or analyze complaints received by agencies on crypto-assets.

List of Figures

www.ingramcontent.com/pod-product-compliance
Lightning Source LLC
Chambersburg PA
CBHW080556220326

41599CB00032B/6502